A BEGINNER'S GUIDE TO THE BIBLE

by
Leo Ward

illustrated by
Peter Dalziel

UNITED KINGDOM TERRITORY
101 Queen Victoria Street, London EC4P 4EP

Commissioner Leo Ward (R)
was commissioned a Salvation Army officer in 1938.
Now retired, his active service was undertaken in the
United Kingdom and Australia. He was Territorial
Commander in Australia Eastern. He served as
Principal at the International Training College and the
International College for Officers. He also served as
Secretary to the Advisory Council to the General at
International Headquarters.

Lieut-Colonel Peter Dalziel
became a Salvation Army officer in 1964 and has since
served in the United Kingdom, South Africa and
Australia. A talented artist, he first developed his
interest in drawing and painting while serving in South
Africa, and in recent years has concentrated on
character studies. He is currently Secretary for
Communications at International Headquarters.

Cover design by Lieut-Colonel Peter Dalziel
Typeset by THQ Print and Design Unit
Printed by WSOY, Finland

A BEGINNER'S GUIDE
TO THE
BIBLE

Contents

General Introduction

Introduction to the Pentateuch

The Books of the Old Testament

The Books of the New Testament

Preface

LIKE a number of books before it, *A beginner's guide to the Bible* began life as a weekly series in the United Kingdom *War Cry*. It was written to order, with the first instalment appearing in print before the third was even written. Once started, there was no going back. The author had committed himself to a punishing schedule – illness, away-from-it-all holidays and writer's block were out of the question for the 66 weeks it would take to complete the task.

As the *War Cry* Editor who commissioned the series, I had a clear concept of what was needed.

The aim of *The War Cry* was, is, and ever shall be to present the Christian gospel to the non-Christian, non-religious woman and man in the street and persuade her or him to give it serious consideration. To do that, fresh-as-paint topical articles are the order of the day.

But on their own these would be a poor diet on which to nourish a questioning mind and a growing religious experience. Those who accept the challenge to launch out in faith need help on their spiritual journey. Above all, they need guidance on how to study the Bible.

Most people on picking up a new book begin at the beginning and read through to the end. That's not a good way to tackle the Bible first time round! If people are going to do that they need a commentary written specifically for that purpose – ideally, one written with the 'typical' *War Cry* reader in mind. None existed. Therefore one would have to be specially written.

I needed to proceed no further than my first choice of writer. A fellow-member of the Sunday congregation at Croydon Citadel, Commissioner Leo Ward, rose to the challenge.

Leo Ward was an inspired choice. His keen-as-mustard mind (unblunted in retirement), coupled with a lifetime's experience of preaching, teaching and living the word of God, produced weekly gems whose scholarship never got in the way of communication.

Great truths were explained, complex themes unravelled, in fewer and simpler words than most of us use to direct a visiting tourist to the railway station. No reader, surely, got lost following Leo Ward's directions!

The series proved a great success. Many appreciative letters were received – including frequent requests for back copies of *The War Cry* covering weeks that had been missed. Many a late-discoverer of the series pleaded for photocopies of 30, 40, 50 previous articles.

Imagine, then, the relief of *The War Cry* Editor's secretary when the decision was taken to publish *A beginner's guide to the Bible* as a book! Such requests could now be met with the promise that the entire series would soon be available.

And here it is. Seen in its entirety it has worth beyond the sum total of its parts. *The War Cry* has not so much lost a weekly series as gained a resource to be recommended without reserve to its readers. I am delighted to have been present at the birth!

Charles King, Captain
Editor, *The War Cry*.

GENERAL INTRODUCTION

THE Bible is like a library containing 66 books of varying sizes, written over a period of more than 1,000 years. Some books mainly record history, others contain prophecy, while a few cover such subjects as Hebrew poetry or wisdom.

The 39 books of the Old Testament record the story of the beginnings and development of the Jewish people and their religion. The New Testament adds the story of the coming of Jesus, his earthly ministry, and the beginnings of the Christian Church.

Various other writings appeared from time to time, but eventually these 66 were selected as revealing special evidence of divine inspiration. They became known as the Canon of Scripture, the word 'canon' meaning a rule, or measure. (A further small group of Jewish writings known as the Apocrypha is included in the Bible used in the Roman Catholic Church.)

Old Testament books were written in Hebrew, New Testament ones in Greek. However, translations soon began to appear to meet the needs of expanding groups of Jews and/or Christians. (It should not be forgotten that until the invention of printing in the 15th century AD, every copy was written by hand, often by groups of monks listening to one of their number reading aloud.)

Translations into English began to appear from around 1,000 AD, but in 1611 King James 1 appointed a group of scholars to prepare a new English translation to be read in the Church of England. This so-called 'Authorised' version gained widespread acceptance and still remains a literary masterpiece of Shakespearean English.

But language is continually changing, and over recent centuries other ancient manuscripts have been discovered, which has led to an increase in the number of translations available for today's reader of English.

The *Good News Bible*, published by the United Bible Societies during the 1960s and 70s, aims, as its foreword states, to 'present the biblical content and message in standard, everyday, natural English'. Based on a simplified vocabulary, it has proved particularly helpful in countries where English has developed alongside the local language. It is this version which is mainly referred to in this book.

Many books are available to assist those who wish to explore the Bible in greater detail. A recently published *Bible Guide*, produced in the Collins Gem pocket edition, contains much helpful material concerning the teaching contained in each book. Many commentaries on individual books have been published and these are readily available in good bookshops.

But it is the reading of the Bible itself which is important. Try and find a quiet place in which you are free from interruption. Pray that the

Holy Spirit will guide you as you read. If a real beginner, start with Mark's Gospel, and also begin to familiarise yourself with the Book of Psalms, with its many prayers and poems.

If possible, have your own Bible in which you can mark verses and passages which are particularly helpful. If your place of worship, or one nearby, has small mid-week Bible study groups, ask for details with a view to joining a group. Informal discussion in an accepting atmosphere often helps in understanding the message.

Always be alert for moments when the words you are reading light up with new and personal meaning for you. As you accept its truth and seek God's help to act upon it, you will find, as many others have done before you, that the Bible really does become 'a lamp to guide me and a light for the path' (Psalm 119:105, *Good News Bible*).

INTRODUCTION TO THE PENTATEUCH

THE name Pentateuch, based on the Greek word for five, refers to the first five books of the Bible, which are specially sacred to the Jewish people, who call them their Torah, or Law.

They are referred to in some Bible translations as the 'Five books of Moses'. This does not mean that Moses actually wrote them all, but as the great founder and architect, under God, of the Jewish national life and its religious code, it is right that his name is linked with this record of the period.

Comments on each individual volume follow in this book, but it may help our understanding to reflect on the long process by which they, and other Old Testament books, were developed.

As with many ancient peoples, stories of their beginnings were kept alive and passed on by word of mouth to each succeeding generation. Then, when writing began, such stories were gathered together and later combined with other oral traditions.

Clues as to the nature of this process can be found within the documents themselves. For example, the author of the Book of Numbers quotes from an earlier book, called 'The Book of the Lord's Battles' (21:14, *Good News Bible*), which has long since been lost.

Again, we sometimes find that an editor has included two separate accounts of the same story from different sources. The Book of Genesis begins with a striking example, by presenting two accounts of the story of Creation. The division between them occurs at 2:4, as clearly indicated in the *Good News Bible*.

Another clue, more difficult to spot, makes it clear that the writer, or editor, is recording happenings from a much earlier date than the time of writing. Thus, in Genesis 36:31, during a somewhat uninteresting piece of writing, the editor says that the kings of Edom, whose names he is listing, reigned 'before there were any kings in Israel'. Obviously that could not have been written before Saul was anointed king over Israel, much later than the time of those Edomite kings!

Other clues have been discovered by scholars who have studied this fascinating subject. When King Josiah (7th century BC) sought to reform the religious life of Judah, he ordered the ruined Temple to be repaired and made ready for use. While this was being done, a 'Book of the Law' was discovered (2 Kings 22). It is believed that much of this book is to be found in the Book of Deuteronomy, now part of the Pentateuch.

Behind the earlier books of the Old Testament, therefore, we can imagine a veritable army of devout Jews patiently gathering together, under the inspiration of the Holy Spirit, the various threads of the unfolding story of God's revelation of himself and his purposes for mankind.

GENESIS

THE word Genesis means 'beginnings'. So, let's make a start. The first 11 chapters form a kind of prologue. You may find three of the stories strange at times, but they speak of important basic truths:

1. The creation of the world

The punchline comes right at the start: 'In the beginning . . . God created the universe.' The beginning of the world was not the result of blind force or the chance meeting of atoms. Creation was the deliberate action of an almighty God.

2. The fall of man

What potential there was for bliss in the Garden of Eden! But it was all forfeited by the decision of the man and woman (Adam and Eve) to disobey the Creator's instructions.

3. Noah and the flood

To what depths of wrongdoing men and women sometimes descend! But God never gives up on mankind. In Noah he found a righteous man, and began again. The rainbow reminds us he always will.

Main theme

Now for the main theme of Genesis. Enter the patriarchs!

Somewhere in northern Syria a tribesman gathers his family and possessions and sets off southwards. Abraham has heard a voice and received a promise. So the story of the ancestors of the Jewish people begins.

Abraham is remembered for his great faith. His son Isaac seems to have been a man of peace. Sadly, Jacob, next in line, deserves the title 'deceiver', for he cheated his brother Esau out of his rightful inheritance.

But the years mature Jacob, and God blesses him with 12 sons. Their experiences – especially those of one of them, Joseph – occupy the last 13 chapters of Genesis.

Joseph's early conceit is changed by his experiences. The brutal treatment, false accusation and imprisonment he suffers prepare him for great responsibility in Egypt as the Pharaoh's right-hand man.

We'll let Joseph have the last word on the stories found in Genesis. To his brothers who stand trembling before him, fearful that he will take revenge on them for their harsh handling of him, he says: 'Don't be afraid. . . . You plotted evil against me, but God turned it into good' (Genesis 50:19, 20, *Good News Bible*).

That says something about the nature of God, don't you think?

EXODUS

IN our look at Genesis, we were introduced to Jacob and his family. We saw how they were at first welcome in Egypt, where Jacob's son Joseph had become an important public figure. Four centuries later, however, they have become a large and growing ethnic minority.

The Book of Exodus opens with Pharaoh's attempts to control the situation: death for all boy babies and slave labour for adults! But he reckons without God, who is planning a different solution.

God already has his 'man for the hour' – Moses – miraculously protected at birth, trained in statecraft right inside Pharaoh's palace but driven into voluntary exile after an abortive attempt to help his fellow Jews.

Then Moses hears God's voice as he stands watching a burning bush. All his excuses for not accepting the task of freeing the Israelites are demolished by God, and Moses returns to Egypt to set about the job. What a contest follows! Pharaoh is determined to hold on to his cheap labour force, but Moses insists that God's command must be obeyed.

A series of devastating plagues reminds Pharaoh that he is dealing with a far greater power than either his own or his god's. So, for the Israelites, release comes at last, and one of history's great migrations begins along the western plains of the Sinai peninsula. (In passing, note the description of the Jewish Passover ceremony. The significance of the Exodus to Jews is seen in the yearly celebration of this festival to this day.)

A series of dramatic adventures ends with a long encampment on the plains below Mount Sinai. There the first steps are taken to weld this company of ex-slaves into a 'nation after God's own heart'.

The Ten Commandments are proclaimed as the foundation of their new national life, and a great ceremony confirms God's covenant, first made to Abraham centuries before.

Throughout all this, Moses is God's representative, moving between mountain and plain to convey the divine requirements.

The incident involving the golden calf reminds us how difficult it is to break away from the past when the going gets tough. But read Moses' moving prayer for his people, and the response from their patient, ever-loving and forgiving God.

The closing chapters describe the making of a portable 'Tent of Meeting' to be carried on later journeys, and some details about the priests, their ceremonial robes and duties. So ends the first stage of the great journey. It will be resumed in a later book.

LEVITICUS

AS the name might suggest, this book contains instructions for Levites (or priests). It might well be called a 'manual of discipline' – a collection of religious and civil laws observed by Jewish people in earlier times.

Thumb through its pages and you may be surprised at some of the subjects covered: aspects of personal hygiene, procedures relating to infectious diseases, references to sexual behaviour, guidance on which animals are considered 'clean' and therefore suitable for food.

A casual reading of what one commentator calls 'this forbidding book' might well give the impression that being a Jew was a burdensome, negative, legalistic way of life. So it could become, as Jesus himself pointed out to some of the narrower-minded Pharisees of his day. But Jesus knew there was more to Jewish life than mere restriction. When challenged to identify 'the greatest commandment', one of the two he chose came from this very book: 'love your neighbour as you love yourself' (19:18, *Good News Bible*).

A closer look at Leviticus reveals the heart that beats beneath the austere framework. Note the compassion to be displayed towards the poor, who on the birth of a baby could offer as a sacrifice a couple of pigeons in place of the usual, more expensive, lamb.

Again, when a farmer gathered his harvest he should not strip the field bare of grain, but leave some for poor people to glean. And if a man fell on such hard times that he had to sell his land, then his brother should come to his aid.

Leviticus contains many details of ceremonies and sacrifices to be observed, together with a description of the role of the priest and of his robes. The book describes an interesting moment in the consecration of a priest, when some of the blood taken from the sacrificial animal is placed on the new priest's right ear, thumb and foot.

There is an echo of this in a Christian hymn written for young people, which includes the words:

> *He claims my hands for active life*
> *In noble deeds and worthy strife;*
> *He claims my feet, that in his ways*
> *I may walk boldly all my days.*

The most important ceremony was the yearly Day of Atonement, a time to remember the people's sins and to celebrate by means of elaborate ritual God's gracious pardon.

Christians see this ancient ceremony as foreshadowing the sacrificial death of Jesus, who on the cross made a 'once and for all' atonement. Through this, Christians believe, all may find forgiveness and restoration to the family of God.

NUMBERS

TWO Bible books ago we looked at Exodus. There we learned how the Israelites escaped from captivity in Egypt and set out on their journey to the Promised Land. Now we turn to the Book of Numbers and find the Israelites continuing that journey.

The book begins with a census taking place during the Israelites' year-long encampment at the foot of Mount Sinai. Its main purpose is to record the names of men, aged 20 and over, eligible for military service.

The Israelites need an army. Being such a large, slow-moving crowd of people, they are constantly at the mercy of marauding bands or hostile armies intent on hindering their progress.

The time comes to break camp and leave Sinai. The Levites are ordered to dismantle the Tent of Meeting, with its special furnishings, and to prepare the Ark of Covenant, containing the precious stone tablets recording the Ten Commandments.

They load everything onto purpose-built wagons, and the second stage of their long march begins. They turn their faces northwards. Ahead is the Promised Land.

Problems *en route*? Of course! There are more complaints about food, even though the manna still falls and quails land near them in abundance. Moses' leadership is challenged once or twice, on one occasion by members of his own family. But eventually stage two is completed. The Israelites arrive at Kadesh Barnea, and another camp is established.

Now it's time to check the way ahead. Twelve men, one from each tribe, are sent to reconnoitre. The report they bring back is mixed.

Fertile? Yes, very! OK to go ahead? Joshua and Caleb say yes, with God's help. But the other 10 say it is too dangerous.

Argument and recrimination follow. The bright promise of the journey's beginning fades away. A long period of purposeless wandering follows before a second attempt is made to find a way through, this time east of the Jordan Valley.

The column skirts around the boundaries of existing kingdoms, facing many tests and trials on the way. Military success gives the Israelites their first tract of land, though not within Canaan itself.

Finally, the Israelites establish a camp within sight of their goal. Across the river lies the city of Jericho and the way ahead.

By now, the entire generation which left Egypt has died, except for Moses, Joshua and Caleb. Preparations begin in earnest for the coming invasion. Moses is still with them, but although it was he who had masterminded the Exodus – braving every danger and opposition on the way – it will not be him who will lead his people into Canaan.

But that story must wait until the next book.

DEUTERONOMY

THE importance of the Book of Deuteronomy is seen in the fact that quotations from it are to be found in no fewer than 17 of the 24 books of the New Testament.

Its influence in an earlier century was no less great. When it was discovered in the ruins of the Jerusalem Temple it initiated one of the most thorough reformations in the history of the Jewish nation.

The name Deuteronomy means Second Law. It is a re-telling of the story of the Exodus and all that followed, presented as a series of addresses given by Moses to his people as they prepared to enter Canaan.

Reminders of the long journey from Egypt occupy the earlier chapters which also include another rendering of the Ten Commandments.

A long central section follows, outlining the 'statutes and ordinances' which are to regulate the worship, daily life and conduct of the Jewish people.

Through what seems at times a tedious recital of things already said, the great principles of a truly godly life are underlined. There is also a reminder of the blessings of obedience and the consequences of rejecting God's plan.

The writer pulls no punches: 'I call heaven and earth to witness the choice you make. Choose life' (30:19, *Good News Bible*). The issue is no less than one of life or death.

In the final chapters the spotlight focuses on Moses, who dominates the story of Israel as recounted in four of the first five books of the Old Testament. The time has now come for him to pass from the stage of earthly history.

In a lengthy psalm, or Hebrew song, the lessons to be learned from the past are summarised. This is followed by a series of blessings on the various tribes.

There are well-loved words here: 'As thy days, so shall thy strength be' (33:25, *Authorised Version*), 'The eternal God is thy refuge, and underneath are the everlasting arms' (33:27, *AV*).

Moses is last seen climbing the slopes of Mount Nebo. From the summit he will be able to view the wide expanse of the Promised Land. But he will not lead his people into it.

Why? The Bible says Moses gave way to anger at a crucial point in the journey. But maybe it is just that his massive task is now done. Another leader, more suited for the battles ahead, must take his place.

'So Moses, the Lord's servant, died there . . . but to this day no one knows the exact place of his burial' (34:5, 6, *GNB*).

A touch of mystery about his passing seems somehow right for this larger-than-life man of God.

JOSHUA

HERE is the first Old Testament book to bear the name of its main character – Joshua. The name is well known. Indeed, we still hear it at times today, though often reduced simply to 'Josh'.

The meaning of the name Joshua, for the Hebrews, was 'The Lord saves!' Its Greek equivalent is Jesus. That should help today's Joshuas stand a bit taller!

Early stories in this book have been popularised in songs such as 'Joshua fit de battle ob Jericho' and 'Deep river; my home is over Jordan'.

Thoughtful readers who delve into the record of these dramatic events need to bear in mind that it is the religious meaning behind the stories which is the writers' overriding interest.

It is their God who makes the river crossing possible at a time of flooding. His is the victory of Jericho (its walls tumbling at the echo of a great shout).

The writers have no doubt that the whole long saga, from the great escape out of Egypt to the assault on Canaan, is the fulfilment of God's divine purpose. In the later words of a psalmist: 'This is the Lord's doing; it is marvellous in our eyes' (Psalm 118:23, *Authorised Version*).

Conversely, failures are attributed finally to human disobedience.

The capture of the town of Ai is an example. In the afterglow of success at Jericho this seems a small challenge which only a few troops can manage. But the Israelite soldiers flee in the face of determined resistance from the inhabitants.

The recorders, however, recognise a deeper truth. When Jericho was captured, one man disobeyed orders and retained some of the spoil for himself. God's army was spiritually weakened by such disobedience, which has to be punished (by the cruel methods of those times) before the failure can be reversed.

So the story continues, with battles fought and won, assemblies affirming the people's loyalty to God and his covenant, and the allotment of territory to the various tribes.

Somehow, though, the vigorous campaign of the early chapters seems to lose momentum. Land is left unclaimed. Perhaps the Israelites are exhausted by the conflicts. It will be many long years before the fruits of God's great purpose begin to be discerned.

Meanwhile, let us remember Joshua, God's faithful soldier.

In the opening words of this book he receives his commission, with the charge: 'Be strong and of a good courage' (1:9, *AV*). He later adds his own unswerving commitment: 'As for me and my house, we will serve the Lord' (24:15, *AV*).

JUDGES

'THERE was no king in Israel . . . Everyone did just as he pleased!' So declares the unknown writer of this book in his closing sentence.

What went wrong? How is it that the dream of a land 'flowing with milk and honey' belonging to God's own chosen people has faded during the almost two centuries following Joshua's death?

The author places the blame squarely on the new generation of Israelites who have forsaken their parents' religion.

They are beguiled by the religion of the Canaanites among whom they live, its fertility rites and other heathen practices. The series of military confrontations they suffer from various quarters is viewed as just punishment for their unfaithfulness to God.

The 'judges' of the title of this book are a group of leaders who, when danger threatens, rally the Israelites to oppose the enemy.

Several also serve for a period as arbitrators in tribal or personal disputes – hence the word 'judge'.

What an oddly-assorted group they are!

Gideon the fearful nevertheless drives out Midianite invaders with just 300 men and a strategy of surprise.

Jephthah, an illegitimate outcast, is recalled to lead his tribe against Ammonite aggressors. Invoking the help of Israel's God, he promises to offer in sacrifice the first person to welcome him home after victory, but is shocked to recognise his own daughter leading the procession!

Strong-man Samson is the best known of the judges. His place in the annals of leadership is no doubt accorded because of his personal exploits against the latest aggressors, the Philistines.

But he sadly fails to fulfil the hopes his parents had when they dedicated him to the Lord. The last of his three love affairs, with Delilah, leads to his betrayal, blinding and imprisonment by his hated foes. In a final act of revenge he brings down the pillars of the heathen temple, killing many Philistines and losing his life.

The closing chapters of Judges tell a sordid story of moral degradation and inter-tribal conflict. No wonder a recent writer describes the book as 'a story of anguish and distress'!

Was it all like this? Was the writer morbidly selective in his choice of material? Did no one remain faithful to the God of Israel and the covenant?

Read the next book for assurance that the light of hope is never quite extinguished, even in the darkest hour.

RUTH

INSTEAD of 'Once upon a time . . .' this delightful love story begins 'In the days when the judges ruled . . .'. This tale of peaceful rural life contrasts with the tragic events and atmosphere of the Book of Judges.

A Jewish couple living in Bethlehem are forced by a famine in Judah to take their two sons and journey to the Land of Moab. There the husband, Elimelech, dies.

His widow, Naomi, is comforted when her sons marry Moabite girls, but sorrow strikes again as each son also dies.

Ten years later, the famine in Judah ends and Naomi decides to return to her native land.

Her two daughters-in-law accompany her as far as the border, from where Naomi assumes they will return home.

They are loath to leave her, but finally one of them turns back. No amount of pleading by Naomi, however, can alter the determination of the other daughter-in-law, Ruth, to remain with her.

Ruth's pledge of lasting devotion has a timeless quality: 'Don't ask me to leave you! . . . Wherever you go, I will go. . . . Your people will be my people, and your God will be my God' (1:16, *Good News Bible*).

True to her word, on arrival in Bethlehem Ruth sets about the task of providing for Naomi and herself.

Eventually, Naomi's kinsfolk come to her aid. One of them, Boaz, buys Naomi's late husband's land, and marries Ruth. He thus fulfils the kinsman's role according to Jewish law and the family line is preserved.

The significance of this is revealed in the closing verses, for the son born to Ruth and Boaz is none other than the grandfather of David, Israel's greatest king.

Indeed, the wider implications of the marriage give Ruth, a young Moabite girl, a place in the ancestry of Jesus.

We could update this lovely story and say: 'In the days of Bosnia, Somalia, South Africa, Northern Ireland . . . .'

In the midst of events which rival those in the Book of Judges for cruelty, tragedy and unfaithfulness, surely there are, in those places, many ordinary people living faithfully according to timeless standards of faith and uprightness.

INTRODUCTION TO PROPHETS
AND PROPHECY

THE prophetic movement in Israel may be said to have begun with Samuel, often described as 'last of the judges, first of the prophets'. His prophetic vocation is shown when he reveals to Saul that his father's lost asses are found, and under divine guidance takes the opportunity to anoint him to be the first King of Israel.

Prophets are popularly believed to have supernatural powers, both to perform miracles and to predict future events. There is some support for this in the Bible, where prophets experience the occasional ecstatic trance, use music to stimulate prophetic activity, experience dramatic visions, and act out object lessons to convey their messages.

But whatever methods may be used, the more important basic fact about them all is their awareness of the reality of God and of his purpose for his people. These are not 'their own men', but servants of God, receiving his message and making it known whatever the reception by their hearers.

During Israel's early monarchy, a prophet is invariably on hand to challenge any king who deviates from the right path. Thus Samuel confronts Saul when he disobeys God's command, Nathan exposes David's wrongdoing by the use of a memorable parable, while Elijah challenges the prophets of Baal to a contest on Mount Carmel to condemn the evil activities of Queen Jezebel.

There are references to 'Schools of the Prophets', notably during the long prophetic ministry of Elisha. Inevitably, false prophets appear, hoping to gain notoriety.

Read the story of the group of court prophets who try to curry favour with their royal patron, King Ahab, by assuring him of a successful end to the military venture he is planning. A lone 'prophet of the Lord', summoned to confirm this, risks his life by declaring a very different result (1 Kings 22). The role of the prophet is no easy ride, often bringing persecution and the threat of death in response to unpopular messages.

A new phase of prophecy begins when, during the 8th century BC, a farmer named Amos travels from Judah into Northern Israel to condemn both king and people for idolatry and their evil treatment of the poor. A collection of his prophecies appears as one of the 15 books of prophecy, which range from major works by Isaiah, Jeremiah and Ezekiel, to several brief treatises. (Jonah is a story about a prophet, rather than a book of prophecy).

Of these men and their prophecies, William Neil says in his one-volume Bible commentary, 'Not all that they said is of equal quality, but among them, and within their collected works, are to be found the men and the ideas that moulded Israel's faith and prepared the way for the coming of Christ and the institution of the Church.'

A long prophetic silence during the period 'between the Testaments' was ended by the appearance of John the Baptist, whom Jesus accepted as fulfilling the prophecy of Malachi 4:5, of a new 'Elijah' who would herald the coming of the promised Messiah (Luke 7:27).

Prophecy continued in the early Christian Church. In the letters of Paul it is referred to as one of the more important gifts of the Spirit (1 Corinthians 12:28). However, it is probable that the emphasis here is on the ability to 'proclaim' the gospel, rather than to 'predict' the future.

FIRST BOOK OF SAMUEL

THE two books of Samuel and two books of Kings provide a more or less continuous story of the Israelite monarchy, which lasted 400 years.

Interwoven throughout are the words and actions of people known as prophets, who advise kings, warn against disobedience towards God, and outspokenly condemn moral failure.

The story begins with Samuel, dedicated at birth to God's service at the temple of Shiloh. He is sometimes called the last of the judges and the first of the prophets.

After a measure of success in uniting the Israelite tribes against Philistine invaders, Samuel loses credibility by appointing his sons as judges, a position they exploit.

The resultant unrest leads to an appeal by tribal elders for the appointment of a king. Samuel's early reluctance is overcome when he receives assurance of divine approval and guidance as to a suitable candidate. So the momentous decision is taken.

Saul, the first king, shows considerable promise, his initial act uniting the tribes against an enemy threatening an Israelite town.

Military action characterises Saul's whole reign, and he achieves some early successes. But military prowess is not to be the only criterion of judgement for Israel's kings. How closely do they obey God's will, and encourage their people to worship and serve him?

On two occasions Saul is judged to have failed this test, so forfeiting the support of Samuel. After the second incident we read, 'As long as Samuel lived, he never again saw the king; but he grieved over him' (15:35, *Good News Bible*).

Samuel is led by God to anoint a successor secretly. And so the youthful shepherd David enters the stage of history. It will be some years before he assumes the throne, but an outburst of popular acclaim greets his early victory over the Philistine giant Goliath.

Saul, troubled and isolated by Samuel's rejection, is consumed with jealousy. As David plays the harp to soothe the king's depression, Saul attempts to kill him. But the young hero flees into the hills and becomes the leader of a band of outlaws whose adventures during his exile make fascinating reading.

Saul's fortunes, meanwhile, are in deep decline. He hunts David without success.

After Samuel's death, and under severe pressure from Philistine invaders, Saul seeks out a medium in the hope of a comforting word from his now-dead mentor, but to no avail. Tragically, Saul is killed in battle against the Philistines, alongside three of his sons.

In his last conversation with David, Saul speaks his own sad epitaph: 'I have been a fool!' (26:21, *GNB*). It might have been so very different.

SECOND BOOK OF SAMUEL

'THE king is dead! Long live the king!' Quite so; but who?

Long ago, Samuel anointed David, but Samuel is now dead. So the stage is set for a struggle over the succession.

The southern tribe of Judah readily accepts David, but among the northern tribes an attempt is made to put Saul's son, Ishbosheth, on the throne.

Seven years of intrigue and conflict follow, until Abner, Saul's former military commander, transfers allegiance to David. Ishbosheth is murdered and David at last is king of a united Israel.

So begins an era of prosperity and expansion.

David's military achievements are impressive, a number of surrounding states being brought within his control, including the troublesome Philistines.

But more important than military success or territorial expansion is the capture of the hill fortress of Jerusalem, which becomes David's capital. It also becomes the nation's religious centre when the Ark of the Covenant, symbol of God's presence, is brought into the city with much pomp and ceremony.

Here we are reminded of David's personal faith in God, as reflected in the many psalms he wrote which brought, and still bring, comfort, consolation and faith to believers everywhere. One of these is included near the end of this book.

Bible writers are open and frank about their heroes, making no attempt to gloss over their failures. In this same book we read of David's tragic love affair with Bathsheba, which calls forth the sternest condemnation from his prophet-adviser, Nathan. Sorrows cloud David's later years, especially the rebellion of his favourite son, Absalom. Troops loyal to David quell the revolt, but Absalom is killed, in spite of an appeal from David.

David's personal faith provides the solid foundation on which his life is built. A strange incident in the final chapter brings the book to a close.

David holds a census of the people. He is told by a prophet that he has done wrong, and must offer sacrifice. Nearby, a wealthy farmer is willing to give David all he needs, including oxen.

David's reply is worthy of careful thought: 'No, I will pay. . . . I will not offer to the Lord my God sacrifices that have cost me nothing' (24:24, *Good News Bible*).

FIRST BOOK OF KINGS

'SOLOMON in all his glory' was Jesus' description of David's personally-chosen successor. Solomon was, as we say, 'born to the purple', inheriting an established administration and a united, prosperous kingdom. As he takes over, all seems set fair for another period of glory.

Solomon's achievements are many. Perhaps the most memorable is the building of the Jewish Temple, its dedication including one of the Bible's noblest prayers for God's blessing.

The magnificence of Solomon's own palace, his vast trading projects, his large army of chariots and horses are all chronicled. They are impressive testimony to his greatness. No wonder the Queen of Sheba, on a state visit, is mightily impressed as she extols the king's great wisdom and prosperity. But on two matters Solomon is not at all wise. To cement alliances with other nations he marries several foreign princesses, in the process opening the door for the introduction of heathen worship, initially for those individuals' benefit.

Solomon's excessive number of wives also adds to the cost of the royal establishment and therefore the burden of taxation to be borne by the people. The people's dissatisfaction grows when forced labour is introduced to carry out the growing number of building projects.

Rumblings of discontent surface. Jeroboam, in charge of the forced labour gangs, is encouraged by the prophet Ahijah to promote rebellion. For this he is exiled to Egypt.

Matters come to a head when Rehoboam, Solomon's son and successor, insolently rejects an appeal from the people to lighten their burdens. Jeroboam hurries back to lead further rebellion, and Rehoboam is forced to flee south, where Judah maintains its loyalty to him as the new king. Jeroboam meanwhile becomes king of the 10 northern tribes, thus bringing an end to a united Israel.

The final chapters of this book record the reigns of various kings, both of north and south. The book summarises their achievements with one of two recurring phrases, saying either 'he did right . . . ' or 'he did evil . . . ' in the sight of the Lord.

It is in these chapters that Elijah – the first of the great prophets – bursts onto the stage to challenge the evils of King Ahab and his foreign queen Jezebel, and to predict their downfall. The prophet's full-throated challenge echoes across the heights of Mount Carmel: 'How much longer will it take you to make up your minds? If the Lord is God, worship him; but if Baal is God, worship him!' (18:21, *Good News Bible*).

As God sends fire from heaven at Elijah's request, the people shout their response: 'The Lord is God; the Lord alone is God!' (18:39, both references from the *GNB*).

SECOND BOOK OF KINGS

THIS action-packed book records the tragic story of the downfall of the Israelite states and the apparent end of the dream which began with those heady moments of escape from slavery in Egypt.

First, read the strange story of the final appearance of the prophet Elijah. Then read about the gracious ministry of Elisha.

Though not of the stature of his illustrious predecessor, Elisha becomes important as a man of the people. Most of his miracles are carried out on behalf of ordinary folk, but one involves the healing of the Syrian military leader, Naaman.

The gathering storm gets worse with the rise of the Assyrian nation, whose capital, Nineveh, stood on the River Tigris in the north of what is now Iraq.

Assyria's rulers conduct campaigns of ruthless terror as they attempt to extend their empire southwards.

The small states in their path, including Israel and Judah, take various measures to resist, sometimes uniting against the Assyrians and sometimes paying them protection money to prevent attack.

Around 730 BC, King Hoshea of northern Israel, having 'paid up' for some years, stops doing so, allegedly with the encouragement of the ruler of Egypt, another of the great powers.

Vengeance quickly follows. Israel is invaded and Hoshea is captured. The Assyrian army then lays siege to Samaria, the capital. After two years' resistance it is captured, and an early form of 'ethnic cleansing' follows. Some 27,000 people are deported to other lands and replaced by other conquered peoples. The Samaritans we read about in the New Testament are descendants of the race of people created by this policy.

The southern kingdom of Judah survives uneasily for another 120 years. Some of its Davidic line of kings heroically endeavour to stem the tide of idolatry which constantly threatens. Other rulers undo all such good work.

A new danger emerges with the defeat of Assyria by the rising power of Babylon.

In the year 597 BC a punitive invasion by the armies of King Nebuchadnezzar results in the deportation to Babylon of 10,000 leaders of Judah, together with their king.

Ten years later a second invasion leaves Jerusalem in ruins and Judah a province of Babylon.

Why did the early dream fade and die? Why did God, who chose Israel, apparently abandon her to her fate? Part of the answer will emerge as we look at the writings of the great prophets.

1 & 2 CHRONICLES

IF you read the same story in several newspapers, you will probably notice differences. These might not be in the facts themselves, but in the interpretation of them, which may reflect the varying interests of the publications.

This happens as we compare Israel's history as recorded in the books of Samuel and Kings with its presentation in the two books of Chronicles, which we now consider.

The 'Chronicler', as he is sometimes called, wrote his history much later than the books of Samuel and Kings were written, perhaps as late as 300 BC. The northern kingdom of Israel had long been overthrown and Judah had also suffered defeat, resulting in captivity and exile for many of its people.

The writer of Chronicles was a member of the priestly class. He may have been an educated scribe, like Ezra, living not under a monarchy but in a small religious community centred on Jerusalem. If so, he would have been controlled by the priests and dominated by the ceremonies and ritual of a restored Temple.

He begins with a series of selected genealogies, demonstrating that God's purpose in creating the Israelites as the people of God reached right back to the creation of Man. (New Bible students shouldn't try to read these first nine chapters at this stage! The story proper begins at chapter 10.) Apart from a brief reference to the death of King Saul, the whole of volume one is given over to the reign of David.

David is clearly the writer's hero and ideal king. He establishes this by omitting events which might tarnish David's image, such as his affair with Bathsheba and the rebellion of Absalom.

Although he acknowledges God's rejection of David's desire to build the first Temple, the writer makes up for this by crediting David with the extensive provision of materials and money, even appointing those who are to provide the services. No less than eight chapters are devoted to this.

The second volume follows the pattern of events described in the earlier history of 1 and 2 Kings. There are special commendations for Hezekiah and Josiah, whose reforms included the re-establishment of Temple worship.

References to the northern kingdom are few, and mostly negative. The writer obviously concludes that it richly deserved its fate. He summarises the closing events of Judah's existence in the final chapter – a sad event deserving the briefest possible reference.

By the way, do read the final two verses of that closing chapter. Note that they are repeated word for word at the commencement of the Book of Ezra which follows. We will consider what that means in the next study.

EZRA

COMPARE the opening verses of the Book of Ezra with the closing words of the previous book and it is immediately obvious that 'The Chronicler' – as he is called – is responsible for both.

Fifty years after the final overthrow of Judah, a dramatic change occurs in the region. Babylonia, one-time conqueror of Assyria, is itself defeated by Cyrus of Persia.

The new ruler's policy towards captive people is very different from that of Assyria or Babylonia. In 539 BC he decrees that exiled people may return, if they wish, to their homelands. It is the Jews' response to this which is described in the books of Ezra and Nehemiah.

Among the leaders of the first group to make the journey home are Zerubbabel, a former governor of the province, and Joshua, the high priest.

Their first task on arrival back in Jerusalem is to set up an altar among the ruins of the old Temple. Next comes plans for the rebuilding of the foundations.

It is a moving moment when everyone gathers to celebrate this event. Shouts of joy mingle with cries of distress from priests old enough to recall the splendour of Solomon's building.

Watching the proceedings are some Jews who have remained in Judah. They offer their help. When this is rejected their interest turns to angry opposition. They appeal to the Persian authorities, who stop the work.

It is some years before a renewed appeal to another king – plus the earnest pleas of two prophets, Haggai and Zechariah – make it possible for a fresh start to be made and the work eventually to be completed.

Not all the Jews return home from exile; perhaps only a minority. Many others are well established and prosperous in their adopted land.

But a further group does return, led by Ezra himself. They include priests and Levites, the organisers of the civil and religious life in the new community.

One problem troubles Ezra above all others. Many of the returned exiles, including leaders, have married non-Jewish women. In chapter nine we read of Ezra's personal distress and of the strong pressures exerted on the offenders, many of whom put away their foreign wives and children. Their names are listed in the final chapter of the book.

Such harsh treatment must be set alongside the undoubted fear that, with Jews now dispersed across the world, the nation chosen by God to fulfil a unique role in the world might lose its identity. That it has not done so, in spite of persecution even in our own century, is a tribute to the faith and tenacity of believing Jews everywhere.

NEHEMIAH

NEHEMIAH was a Jew who had risen to service in the household of King Artaxerxes in Babylon, becoming his personal wine steward. His brother Hanani, returning from a visit to Judah, brings disturbing news of slow progress in Jerusalem. The walls are still in ruins and the gates still broken down.

Nehemiah's distress at the news is noticed by the king. When he learns the cause, he gives Nehemiah leave of absence to travel to Jerusalem to see the situation for himself.

So begins a remarkable story of energetic and prayer-charged action which revitalises the dispirited community.

Nehemiah's personal diary, freely used by the author of this book, tells of his secret night-time inspection of the ruins, then of his meeting with local leaders. As Nehemiah unfolds his plans, the leaders are stirred to action. Priests, officials and leaders join in the mammoth task, each family or group being assigned to repair a section of the wall, or one of the gates.

Opposition from local groups, Samaritans and others soon emerges. Ridicule and threats are levelled at the builders.

They have other problems too. The piles of rubble seem unending, and their aching limbs rebel at the demands made on them.

Nehemiah's diary records, 'I didn't take off my clothes even at night . . . we all kept our weapons to hand' (4:23, *Good News Bible*).

The opposition includes a rumoured attempt on Nehemiah's life. To this he makes the curt reply: 'I'm not the kind of man who runs and hides!'

In spite of the difficulties, Jerusalem's walls are completed in 52 days amid great rejoicing.

The people come together for a ceremony of dedication. It begins with a reading from the Law of Moses by Ezra the scribe, followed by the Festival of Shelters, a reminder of the desert wanderings of long ago, and concludes with a covenant-signing ceremony. During this, Nehemiah, as Governor, is the first of a long list of representative leaders who sign the document.

Some years later Nehemiah, on a second visit to Judah, discovers that abuses are again creeping in. They include non-payment of tithes of grain for the Temple, trading on the Sabbath and more cases of marriage to foreign wives.

Nehemiah angrily takes strong action to change the situation. His despair at such evidence of human weakness is reflected in the prayer with which his diary closes: 'Remember all this, O God, and give me credit for it!' (13:30, *GNB*). He has done his best.

ESTHER

HAVING briefly studied the books which recount Israel's chequered history, we now turn to other kinds of Bible literature.

The Book of Esther tells a colourful and dramatic story. It begins with the dismissal by King Xerxes of Persia of his queen, Vashti, for disobeying a summons to 'show her beauty' before his carousing guests.

The search for a beautiful young woman to take her place ends when Esther, a Jewess, is chosen. On the advice of her guardian, Mordecai, who is also a palace official, her race is not disclosed at first.

Enter the villain, Haman the prime minister, a pompous individual who, with the king's backing, demands that all lesser officials kneel and bow to him.

Mordecai the Jew refuses to do so. Angered by this, Haman manoeuvres the king into signing a royal decree condemning 'a certain race of people' (the Jews, of course) to be exterminated.

Mordecai, much distressed at the news, sends word to Esther. At a banquet attended by both king and prime minister, Esther exposes Haman's treachery and pleads for the lives of her people.

A second decree is then drawn up, permitting the Jews to defend themselves when attacked. This saves the lives of many of them.

Why is this story in the Bible? The name of God is never mentioned, and indeed it was one of the last books to be accepted into the Hebrew scriptures.

However, through it we learn again of God's care for his people when danger threatens. We also note Mordecai's word to Queen Esther that her choice as queen may well have been providential, since she alone could save her people from their fate.

Esther, in turn, deserves admiration for her great courage in approaching the king without first being summoned into his presence.

Near the end of the book it is suggested that a Jewish feast known as Purim may owe its existence to the celebrations following the Jews' victory, a possible reason for the book's inclusion in the Bible.

By the way, don't miss the story, in chapter 6, of Haman's humiliation when ordered by the king to escort Mordecai on a triumphal parade through the city streets. It is a wonderfully ironic situation, proving the Bible has its lighter moments!

JOB

THIS book has been described as among the greatest masterpieces of world literature. It is mainly a work of poetry. Modern translations indicate this by changing from prose to poetry form at verse two of chapter 3 and back again at verse 2 of chapter 42.

Job himself is described as a good and upright man with a large family and much wealth. His situation is discussed in an imaginary 'heavenly council'.

Satan (or Adversary), when speaking to God, claims Job's goodness is just a ploy to secure divine favour. Let him lose everything and he'll soon change his tune!

Permission is given for this to happen, and a series of disasters is graphically described, with Job's animals, servants, and finally sons and daughters destroyed.

Job's sorrowing reply to such catastrophe is well known: 'The Lord gave, and now he has taken away. May his name be praised!' (1:21, *Good News Bible*).

Satan's second assault is to cover Job's body with 'loathsome sores' so that even his wife retorts, 'Why don't you curse God and die?'

Three friends – Eliphaz, Bildad, and Zophar, his 'comforters' – arrive and sit with him in silence until Job breaks into a mournful lament concerning his condition. Then dialogue begins.

Each friend speaks three times, trying variously to explain his condition. Perhaps Job's children are at fault, or perhaps he needs discipline?

Their sympathy passes to accusation. Job must have committed sin. He is blaspheming God by his words. His only solution is to confess and submit to God in penitence.

Job's response is by no means passive. He chides his 'friends' for failing him in his hour of need, even charging God himself with being capricious and refusing to listen. A fourth friend's intervention adds nothing new to the conversation.

At last the voice of God is heard 'out of the storm'. In four magnificent chapters Job is treated to a vivid description of the created world, which leaves him helpless and penitent for even daring to question such a God!

The book concludes, perhaps rather lamely, with Job's restoration to health and an even better life than he enjoyed before.

What, then, may we learn from this story? Certainly, that suffering is not necessarily the result of wrongdoing.

The deeper question, 'Why do good people suffer?' is not really addressed.

But at the heart of the book is a clue to a truth given prominence in the New Testament. What if there is life beyond the grave? Is it possible that undeserved suffering *here* will be balanced by blessing *there*?

In chapter 19 the tortured Job expresses such a hope, which can be read in verses 25 to 27. Better still, it can be heard on tape or disc as a glorious soprano voice (Isobel Baillie for me!) sings the sublime aria from Handel's *Messiah:*

> *I know that my Redeemer liveth . . .*
> *And though worms destroy this body,*
> *Yet in my flesh I shall see God!*

That ancient poet surely had something there!

PSALMS

SONGS appeared early in Jewish history. Two examples are when Miriam danced and sang to celebrate the Red Sea crossing, and when Deborah recorded in song the Israelites' victory over Sisera's army. Later, the existence of the monarchy and the building of the Temple gave new impetus to the use of songs as aids to worship.

The Book of Psalms is sometimes called 'The Hymn Book of the Second Temple'. This suggests that its production was well advanced by the time groups of Jews returning from exile in Babylon began re-establishing worship in the rebuilt Temple.

The *Good News Bible* is among several modern translations which indicate how the Jews divided the book into five sections, each concluding with a doxology. For illustration see Psalm 41:13. The result is a sort of 'Pentateuch of Praise' to match the 'Pentateuch of Law' comprising the first five books of the Old Testament.

The *Good News Bible* also provides a heading for each psalm, illustrating the variety of subjects covered.

The predominant theme is praise and thanksgiving to God for the wonders of creation, and for personal and national blessings. But many psalms are cries from the heart for help in trouble or perplexity.

From the subject matter itself, or from notes added by the compilers, it is possible to determine the event which gave rise to a particular psalm's composition. Psalm 42, for instance, reflects the exile experience, while Psalm 45 was doubtless sung at a royal wedding.

Many psalms are attributed to David, who is described in 2 Samuel 23:1 as 'the composer of beautiful songs for Israel'.

David's skill with the harp may also have stimulated the use of musical instruments for accompaniment.

Several psalms are ascribed to other authors, while many remain anonymous. The poetic form in which the psalms are written is known as 'parallelism', each couplet of two lines expressing either similar truths in different words, or sometimes contrasting truths. The *Good News Bible* version brings this out clearly (Psalm 18, for example).

These brief introductory notes cannot convey the beauty of language or depth of spiritual insight expressed in the psalms. Only a quiet, thoughtful reading will release their treasures to minister to your heart and mine.

So, how about beginning with the best-known and best-loved 23rd Psalm: 'The Lord is my shepherd'?

You could then turn to Psalm 27: 'The Lord is my light and my salvation' and then Psalm 46: 'God is our shelter and strength' (all references from the *Good News Bible*).

From these three psalms alone you will surely begin to discover the rich blessings available in these 150 songs!

PROVERBS

'A STITCH in time saves nine.' Yes, that's a proverb. So is 'Too many cooks spoil the broth.' Many such phrases expressing practical advice on 1,001 subjects have passed into our language.

In this study we look at the Bible's own collection – the Book of Proverbs. Compiled from several ancient sources, the book has a unique ingredient – practical, down-to-earth wisdom regarding faith in the reality and goodness of God. For the writers of the Book of Proverbs, reverence for God is the beginning of wisdom.

A modern commentator suggests a simple motto to sum up the book's basic message: 'Trust in God and do the right.'

The name of King Solomon appears at the book's beginning. Solomon is regarded as having stimulated the development of what is called Hebrew Wisdom literature, examples of which are Job, Proverbs and Ecclesiastes.

The historical book of 1 Kings credits Solomon with composing 3,000 proverbs and more than 1,000 songs!

The first lengthy section of Proverbs is presented as advice from a father to his son. There are things for the young man to avoid: evil companionship, laziness, dishonesty, immorality. In contrast, there are qualities to cultivate: loyalty, faithfulness, integrity, care for the needy.

Included here is a poem 'In praise of wisdom', similar in content and style to chapter 28 of the Book of Job.

The main central section of Proverbs consists of two groups of sayings, said to be written by Solomon. The second group appears to have been gathered by officials at the court of Hezekiah, who lived some two centuries after Solomon's death.

Note the use of the Hebrew form of poetry known as parallelism. The first verse of chapter 10 is a good example: 'A wise son makes his father proud of him; a foolish one brings his mother grief' (*Good News Bible*).

Proverbs is not a book to read curled up in an armchair in front of the fire with an hour to spare. It's to be dipped into occasionally and enjoyed for its picturesque and sometimes humorous language. This is enhanced in the illustrated *Good News Bible* by the miniature line drawings by the Swiss artist Annie Vallotton.

When reading the description, in the final chapter, of what constitutes a 'capable wife' you may be tempted to agree with the opening phrase that such a 'perfect' person is hard to find!

Better, though, to conclude that times have changed, and acknowledge that the description needs updating in the light of the more 'level playing field' enjoyed by many modern-day couples. Today's equality more than compensates for the reduced 'servant' role of earlier generations!

ECCLESIASTES

THE author of this third Old Testament book of wisdom is unknown. He styles himself 'David's son who was king in Jerusalem', which suggests he is Solomon. However, while Solomon is recognised for his involvement in Wisdom literature, in the case of Ecclesiastes it's generally agreed that his name has simply been borrowed to give the work greater acceptance.

Whoever the author is (the book refers to him as 'the preacher'), he thinks long and deeply about the meaning of life with its varied components. But he seems to notice mostly the dark colours in the spectrum of life. He has indeed hardly begun to write before he introduces his motto/theme: 'Vanity of vanities . . . all is vanity!' (1:2, *Authorised Version*). He tells of his own attempts to find the key to satisfaction, first by the exercise of great power and authority. Then he works to amass great possessions – house, vineyards, slaves and so on.

He then tries to cheer himself up by indulging in a giddy round of pleasures. But with what overall conclusion? Yes, you've guessed it: 'It is all useless. It is like chasing the wind' (2:26, *Good News Bible*).

One of the often-quoted passages in the book describes the unending round of life's experiences: times of birth and death, times of sorrow and joy, of loving and hating, seeking and finding, and so on.

These, he concludes, are ordained by God, and we cannot change them. Our only recourse is to accept what comes along and as far as possible enjoy it. The preacher is strongly aware of the reality of God, whom to obey is to 'do right' and to disobey is to merit condemnation. At the same time, as with other writers on this subject, he is frankly perplexed by life's injustices. 'Look at what happens in the world: sometimes righteous men get the punishment of the wicked, and wicked men get the reward of the righteous' (8:14, *GNB*).

He has no answer to this problem. Indeed, his perplexity is increased because he can find no reason to believe in life after death. 'No one can tell us what will happen after we die' (10:14, *GNB*).

Even when, in the closing chapter, he writes what has been described as 'a super allegory of the onset of old age' he cannot break out of his pessimistic mould, warning: 'Remember your Creator while you are still young' (12:1, *GNB*).

Why did Ecclesiastes find a place in the Bible? It is at times valuable to take a frank and solemn look at the more serious side of life, but only as long as it is seen as merely a part of the overall 'colour scheme' God has planned for his children, and as long as life's eventual sunset is seen as just a prelude to the dawning of a new and glorious day.

This, in contrast to the somewhat morbid writer of Ecclesiastes, is what today's 'preachers' delight to proclaim.

SONG OF SOLOMON

THE Bible book known as the Song of Solomon (or Song of Songs) is an unusual work – a collection of love poems. The book provides further testimony to King Solomon's influence on Hebrew literature. He's not the author, but he is one of the characters in the poems.

The unknown writer skilfully colours his work with a tapestry of scenes from country life. Sheep and goats graze among the hills or rest in the shade from the noonday sun. Birdsong is heard everywhere, while gazelles, stags and foxes bound across the fields and through the vineyards. Lilies and other wild flowers cover the hillside and the air is heavy with the scent of herbs.

What is it all about?

Several suggestions have been made. The simplest is the one put forward in the *Good News Bible*.

A man, named as King Solomon, and a beautiful peasant girl express their love for each other in highly emotive language. Their joy in each other's company and their appreciation of each other's physical excellence are described in poems of great beauty. Brief 'choruses' spoken or sung by a group of women are inserted.

Another suggestion is based on a stronger story-line. It has three characters, not two – the king and the girl as before, and a young shepherd who loves the girl deeply.

The shepherd is heartbroken when the girl is taken to the palace. He sets out to find her, hoping to persuade her to return to him and to the simple life of the country.

Eventually she does so, and the playlet ends with further poems expressing their undying love for each other.

Now, if the work is no more than a dialogue extolling human love, why was its message – however commendable – considered worthy of a place in the Bible?

The answer is surprisingly simple. Jewish scholars, recognising the beauty of the love expressed (and no doubt noting the reference to King Solomon), saw in it a reflection of God's love for his people, Israel.

Not only did they include it in their Scriptures, they also chose it to be read during the solemn Passover festival.

Christians have similarly accepted the message as one describing the loving relationship between Christ and his Church. But let's not lose sight of the simpler message about the idyllic love between a man and a woman, and of the happiness they find in each other.

In this day of shifting values, when relationships are often frivolous, shallow and passing, the Bible still declares that ideals like loyalty, fidelity and trust are capable of creating a relationship of enduring worth. As such they are worthy of emulation by us all.

27

ISAIAH (chapters 1-39)

PROPHETS have appeared in earlier books of the Bible. Men like Samuel, Nathan and Elijah fearlessly rebuked kings for disobedience to the Lord. Prophets of this later time, in addition to words and actions, left a remarkable written record of their messages which have inspired God's people ever since. A simple phrase sums up the prophet's vocation: 'Thus says the Lord!'

The book bearing the name of Isaiah is thought to be a collection of messages by several authors from different periods in Israel's history, brought together over many years by disciples and successors of the man we know as 'Isaiah of Jerusalem'. He lived there with his wife and two sons during the reigns of four of Israel's kings over a period of more than 50 years. It is in the first 39 chapters of the book that we find his own contributions.

He describes his call to the prophetic vocation in chapter six. In the Temple one day, he is acutely aware of the presence of God 'high and lifted up' filling the whole building. Impressed with a sense of the holiness of God, he confesses his own and his people's uncleanness. But he receives cleansing, and responds positively to the call to become God's special messenger to his people.

That vision of God's holiness stimulates the prophet's early messages of stern condemnation for the people's mixing of true and false religion, and for evil conduct of many kinds. Describing the nation as 'God's special vineyard', he insists that the only fruit produced is 'sour grapes'. What if God should remove the boundary fences?

Isaiah's advice to Kings Ahaz and Hezekiah is to avoid alliances with heathen nations and put their trust wholly in God. The former rejects the advice and suffers for it, while the latter accepts and Jerusalem is saved.

As you read and try to grasp the meaning behind the colourful symbolic language, look out for Isaiah's two positive themes. He foresees the possible break-up of the nation, but his unbounded faith in God leads him to believe that a surviving 'remnant' will continue to be true to God. (Note the symbolic name given to one of his sons in chapter 7 verse 3.)

More than that, he believes that the glorious days of King David's reign will one day be repeated in even greater fashion. A new 'David' will be born, a descendant in the Davidic line, through whom blessing will come not only upon Israel but on all humankind: 'For unto us a child is born . . . his name shall be called Wonderful, Counsellor . . . Prince of Peace . . .' (9:6, *Authorised Version*).

Though he may not have fully realised it, Isaiah initiated one of the Old Testament's greatest revelations, which would be fulfilled by the birth of a baby in Bethlehem.

ISAIAH (chapters 40-66)

CHAPTER 40 of the Book of Isaiah marks a significant high peak in biblical revelation. The unknown writer looks out on a situation much changed from that of 'Isaiah of Jerusalem', the author of the book's first 39 chapters.

Judah and its capital are no more. Assyria, cruel scourge of small states, has been defeated by Babylon, which in turn is conquered by King Cyrus of Persia. Cyrus's enlightened policy, decreed in 539 BC, permits captives who wish to do so to return to their homeland.

It is against this promising background that a new and positive note is sounded: 'Comfort my people . . . they have suffered enough . . . clear the way . . . remove every obstacle . . . let them prepare to return home!' The author breaks into a sublime poetic description of the greatness of God, who, like a shepherd, is ready to gather his people like sheep and lambs under his protection and lead them home. In a memorable closing segment, the people are assured of God's loving care for the young, the weak and the old, who will 'walk and not faint'. These and other themes are developed in the chapters that follow.

'God is one, and God alone' is stated again and again. 'Beside me there is no other God; there never was and there never will be!'

In contrast, the prophet holds up to ridicule the makers of idols who from the same tree make a fire for warmth and a god to worship.

Prophesying the utter defeat of Babylon, the prophet presents a picture of the Israelites loading the Babylonians' gods on to wagons to be carted away, their magicians and astrologers having been exposed as false.

Scholars have identified within these chapters four poems which they call 'Songs of the servant'. The poems are not easily identified in English translations of Isaiah, but the first – in chapter 42 – begins: 'Here is my servant whom I have chosen.'

The fourth, and greatest, begins at 52:13 and includes the whole of chapter 53. The servant here suffers rejection, pain and death, but secures forgiveness and healing for his sinful people.

Christians find in this moving passage a description of Jesus, who, as the hymn writer says, 'died that we might be forgiven'.

From chapter 56 to the end a further set of prophecies might relate to an even later time, when some Jews are back in Judah.

Appeals to turn from sinful ways are again heard, but there are also passages of great beauty, containing great promises.

It was from this section that Jesus chose the theme with which to announce his public ministry: 'The sovereign Lord has . . . chosen me and sent me to bring good news to the poor' (61:1, *Good News Bible*).

There could be no better link between the *promise* of the Old Testament and the *fulfilment* of the New (see Luke 4:18, 19).

JEREMIAH

JEREMIAH, a member of a priestly family, begins his ministry in the reign of the last reforming king of Judah, King Josiah.

The prophet supports the reformation, but after the king's untimely death in battle, there is no other like-minded ruler, and things go from bad to worse.

In 597 BC, King Nebuchadnezzar of Babylon invades Judah, taking the king's son and many leading citizens into exile in Babylon. Ten years later he returns, this time besieging and capturing Jerusalem and taking more Jews into captivity.

Through all these events Jeremiah remains in Jerusalem, supported by his faithful scribe, Baruch.

His constant appeal is for the people to change their ways, give up idolatry and evil, and return to the Lord. He has no doubt about the tragic consequences which will follow their rejection of God's plan for Israel.

Jeremiah, a shy and sensitive man, endures much suffering and ill treatment because of his unpopular messages. He is flogged, placed in the stocks and exposed to ridicule.

When Jerusalem is attacked, Jeremiah is imprisoned on the orders of King Zedekiah, who fears the effect of his preaching on morale in the city.

During a pause in the siege Jeremiah sets out to visit relatives living nearby, but is spotted and seized by a sentry for 'deserting to the enemy'.

As the fighting reaches its climax Jeremiah is flung into a pit, and survives only by the intervention of a friendly foreigner.

Jeremiah loves his people and suffers greatly because of the stern messages he is given to proclaim.

In several moving passages he confesses his anguish, cursing the day he was born, and vowing to give up his ministry.

Then he recalls: 'Your message is like a fire burning deep within me. I try my best to hold it in, but can no longer keep it back' (20:9, *Good News Bible*).

No wonder Jeremiah is known as the man of sorrows of the Old Testament!

The severity of his predictions does not mean that Jeremiah believes Judah is finished as a nation.

Scattered throughout his book are passages bright with hope for the future.

Read the letter Jeremiah writes to the first group of captives away in Babylon (chapter 29), and the promises of restoration which follow in chapters 30 to 33. (Note the story of his purchase of a field from a relative as a sign of his faith in the future.)

Also found in this segment is Jeremiah's greatest contribution to scriptural truth.

He speaks of God's covenant through Moses, based on obedience to written laws which the people are failing to keep.

Jeremiah then describes his 'New Covenant' which God will initiate, involving an inward change of life.

It will be a 'Covenant of the heart' ensuring a new and more permanent relationship of love and devotion between God and his people. This covenant, Christians believe, was sealed by the life and sacrificial death of Jesus – a new covenant, a new testament, indeed!

LAMENTATIONS

IN the Book of Jeremiah we read a description of the tragic overthrow of Judah and the destruction of its holy city, Jerusalem. In Lamentations we have – as the title suggests – a moving 'lament for a lost city'. Each of the five chapters is a poem. The first four are constructed in a special form sometimes used in Hebrew poetry, where the 22 verses begin with the consecutive letters of the Hebrew alphabet. This, of course, is lost in the translation into English.

Whether Jeremiah wrote these poems is unclear, but they convey their message in language of great beauty. The language accentuates the bitter sadness and despair of the subject:

The noblest of cities has fallen . . . the towers and walls now lie in ruins . . . Jerusalem's old men sit on the ground in silence . . . children and babies are fainting in the streets . . . O Jerusalem, beloved Jerusalem, what can I say? How can I comfort you? (1:1; 2:8, 10, 11, 13, all quotations from the *Good News Bible*).

In the third poem the writer is reminded of his own personal experience during the disaster:

I cry aloud for help, but God refuses to listen; I stagger as I walk . . . People laugh at me . . . I have forgotten what health and peace and happiness are (3:8, 9, 14, 17).

Yet in the middle of reciting his many troubles, a truth he had forgotten reawakens in him:

Hope returns when I remember this one thing: The Lord's unfailing love and mercy still continue, fresh as the morning, as sure as the sunrise (3:21-23).

The recollection of this 'star of hope' shining in the black night of his despair encourages the poet to appeal to his countrymen:

Let us examine our ways . . . let us open our hearts to God in heaven and pray (3:40, 41).

The final two poems return to the tragedy of it all, with even more lurid pictures of suffering and grief:

Hunger has made us burn with fever . . . Our wives have been raped . . . Our leaders have been taken and hanged . . . our young men are forced to grind corn like slaves . . . Happiness has gone out of our lives; grief has taken the place of our dances (5:10-15).

In the closing verses, however, the writer, in a moving appeal, turns to the Lord, who alone can break through the darkness:

But you, O Lord, are king for ever . . . Bring us back to you, Lord! . . . Restore our ancient glory (5:19-21).

God did so. And he always will in response to the truly penitent in heart. As today's Christians sing, inspired by an earlier translation of a verse highlighted above:

Great is thy faithfulness, Lord, unto me!

EZEKIEL

MANY leading citizens are taken captive to Babylon when Nebuchadnezzar's army first marches into Judah in 597/8 BC. Among them is a young priest, Ezekiel.

Five years later Ezekiel receives a strange and complex vision of the 'glory of the Lord'. Ezekiel is addressed as 'son of man', appointed as watchman to his countrymen and presented with a scroll containing writing. Ezekiel is to 'eat' it. In other words, thoroughly digest its message and make it known.

The prophet declares that Jerusalem's sufferings are not yet over. Using visual aids, he draws on a tile the outline of a city under siege, complete with battering-rams and other implements.

Ezekiel cuts off his hair and divides it into segments, indicating the various sufferings the inhabitants will sustain, as commanded by the Lord. In the middle of warning about the judgement that is to come on the people for their sinfulness, Ezekiel seems to find himself once more in Jerusalem. It is as if he is a 'fly on the wall', observing at first hand the dreadful happenings taking place in the very precincts of the Temple. His vision ends with the 'glory of the Lord' departing.

Eventually the prophet proclaims that the siege of Jerusalem has begun. Two years later, news of its final destruction is reported by a man who escaped from the ruins.

Now the mood of Ezekiel's message changes from condemnation to hope and promise, as he prepares the exiles for eventual return to Judah. In place of their faithless leaders (or shepherds) God will provide a shepherd of his own choice. He will be another David, the beloved shepherd-king of earlier days.

To fit the people for the task ahead Ezekiel promises, as Jeremiah did before him, that God will give them 'a new heart' and 'a new spirit'. To emphasise this promise Ezekiel describes a vision of a valley of dry bones. First the scattered bones form themselves into skeletons, then flesh forms on them and finally they are given new life by the breath of the Spirit of God. A living army!

The last nine chapters describe in elaborate detail a blueprint for the new Temple in the new city, to which God's glory will return.

Near the end of the book, in perhaps his greatest vision, Ezekiel observes a river. This 'River of Life' emerges as a tiny stream from beneath the altar of the new Temple then quickly deepens as it spreads across the country. Eventually it reaches the dry, salty basin of the Dead Sea, having dispensed sweetness and life all along the way.

Though much has happened to challenge such a promising picture, God's people continue to believe that this 'holy, mighty, wonder-working river' (as the old hymn has it) flows on to refresh the life of today's world.

DANIEL

DANIEL is a Bible character best known for surviving, unharmed, a night in a den of lions. Three of his friends are similarly renowned for living to tell the tale after being thrown into a burning fiery furnace following their refusal to deny their Hebrew faith.

These dramatic events, which took place during the Jews' exile in Babylon during the sixth century BC, are described in the first six chapters of the Book of Daniel. In the following six chapters there are other strange stories and mysterious language. How do the two sections of the book fit together, and what can we make of them? The vision described in chapter seven provides an important clue. Briefly, it tells of four beasts which rise out of a stormy sea – a lion, a bear, a leopard, and finally a terrifying beast with 10 horns.

The four represent successive world powers – Babylonia, Media, Persia and Greece. When Alexander the Great died young, his empire was divided. One part was then ruled from Syria, and the 10 horns represent its kings.

The 'little horn' mentioned in verse eight is identified as Antiochus IV, whose evil reign over the same area in the second century BC threatened to destroy the Jewish state and its religion. It was probably during this reign that the Book of Daniel was written.

Unfortunately, the history of the period is not told in the Bible, though it can be read in the books of 1 and 2 Maccabees, included in some modern translations (*The Jerusalem Bible*, for example).

Antiochus set out to unify the countries under his control by promoting Greek culture – its language, dress and lifestyle. Meeting strong opposition from some Jews, he determined to impose his will, forbidding sacrifice on any but heathen altars and forbidding possession of the Jewish scriptures.

The crunch came when a heathen altar to Zeus was set up in the Jewish temple itself. A priest named Mattathias, together with his five sons, became the focus of growing resistance. Such was the effect of this that under Judas, nicknamed 'The Hammerer', the enemy was defeated and the temple cleansed and rededicated for worship in 165 BC. It was during the three-and-a-half years of this bitter struggle that the Book of Daniel was written.

It begins with the stirring events of the exile years, extolling the courage and faithfulness of Daniel and his friends. Then, from chapter seven onwards, the unknown writer – using visions as a kind of secret code – portrays the struggle of his own time, calling his fellow Jews to meet their present challenges with the same courage.

Yes, much of the book is difficult to understand, but its message is timeless and applicable to every age when God's people are threatened by evil.

HOSEA

THE last 12 books of the Old Testament are named after men who are often referred to as the 'minor' prophets. This is not because they are necessarily less important but because the books named after them are brief compared with those dealing with the three 'major' prophets which precede them.

Unfortunately, the 12 books do not appear in chronological order, so a brief word on the historical background of each will be necessary.

Hosea appears about 200 years before the Jews' return from exile. The two nations of Northern Israel and Southern Judah are in existence.

A brief respite from the warring attentions of Assyria and Egypt enables both nations, under Jeroboam II of Israel and Uzziah of Judah, to achieve territorial gains and commercial success, though the result is far from God-honouring.

Focusing on the northern kingdom we see a wealthy merchant class becoming so corrupt by its lust for riches that its members ignore Jewish law and exploit the helplessness of the poor. As so often happens, religion becomes a mere formality, corrupted by the introduction of aspects of Baal worship.

Into this situation come two prophets, Amos and Hosea.

Hosea is an Israelite, and his family life provides illustrations for his message. His three children, for example, are given symbolic names which reflect some of Hosea's sterner themes.

Again and again Hosea reminds his people of God's past judgements on their disobedience and warns that they risk forfeiting God's mercy and losing their place as his chosen people.

Hosea's tragic marriage also becomes a kind of 'text' which illustrates a great truth.

From the first three chapters of the Book of Hosea we learn that Hosea's wife, Gomer, is unfaithful, leaving him for other lovers and eventually becoming a prostitute.

Gomer's degradation is complete when she is put up for sale in a slave market. When Hosea hears of this, he goes in search of Gomer, pays the required price and brings her back home.

If Hosea can show such love and compassion towards his unfaithful wife, surely God will do no less for his seriously erring people?

Side by side with words of stern condemnation we read beautiful promises of hope, such as those found in chapter 2 verses 14-23 and in the poetic sections of chapter 11.

Indeed, this aspect of Hosea's message is so important that it inspires the prophet's closing words: 'I will bring my people back ... love them with all my heart ... answer their prayers and take care of them' (14:4, 8, *Good News Bible*).

Regretfully, Hosea does not see the fulfilment of his hopes. Indeed, he may well have lived to witness the violent destruction of his nation by Assyria. But we are still inspired by Hosea's picture of God, who, while condemning human sinfulness, offers mercy and compassion. Christians believe God is the same today!

JOEL

THE Book of Joel begins with his prophetic outburst, inspired by a devastating plague of locusts. He describes the swarms of grasshopper-like insects as a great army, blotting out the sun as they swoop, wave upon wave, to settle on everything green.

Crops, grapevines, fig trees – nothing escapes the locusts' ravaging hunger as they systematically chew away every living morsel, leaving only dry stalks and bare tree-trunks.

The tragedy is compounded as a severe drought empties the streams, and the ground dries hard in the searing sun.

Such destruction reminds Joel of 'the day of the Lord'. He calls the people to sincere repentance for their sinful ways: 'Rend your hearts and not your garments,' he tells them.

Everyone, old and young, even babies, must gather in the Temple. The priests who 'serve between the altar and the porch' are to lead the congregation in prayer and confession. Perhaps the Lord will be gracious and forgive their sins.

In an abrupt change of tone, Joel gives voice to his belief that the plague is ending. The swarms appear to be moving away. There are signs that seasonal rains are coming again, to fill the streams, quench the animals' thirst and cause the crops to grow. 'Be glad, people of Zion. Rejoice at what the Lord has done for you!' he says.

Joel reminds the people of the promise voiced earlier by Jeremiah and Ezekiel, relating to the time when the Lord will pour out his Spirit upon everyone who trusts in him, delivering them from their troubles.

Unfortunately, as we read on into the third chapter, the prophet reveals a narrow, nationalistic vision. Joel imagines the nations which have afflicted Israel being summoned to face the Lord in 'The valley of judgement'.

In a strange reversal of the lovely promise of Isaiah and Micah, Joel calls the people to 'hammer your ploughs into swords, and your pruning knives into spears' in order to face the Lord's army. But the issue is never in doubt. For Joel, all those heathen nations will be destroyed. His blinkered vision can see a place in God's purpose only for repentant Israel. It is left to the apostle Peter – some four centuries later, when he addresses the crowd that gathers on the Day of Pentecost – to quote Joel's promise of the outpouring of the Lord's Spirit, and give it wider meaning.

The promise is indeed for everyone. Not Jews alone, but men, women and children from every nation. All who hear and respond to God's gracious invitation can join his redeemed family.

The truth of Joel's great promise finally becomes clear to Peter through the ministry of Jesus, who declares, 'I will never turn away anyone who comes to me.'

AMOS

CHRONOLOGICALLY Amos is the earliest of the 'minor' prophets. Unlike Hosea, he is a citizen not of northern Israel but of southern Judah – which guarantees a poor reception for his message in the north.

(On one occasion, described in chapter 7 verse 12, Amos meets a priest presiding at the shrine at Bethel who turns on the unwelcome visitor with the words: 'That's enough, prophet! Go back to Judah and do your preaching there!')

Amos begins his prophecy by surveying the overall scene, giving brief glimpses of Israel's neighbouring states such as Syria, Philistia and Tyre.

The failings of each are summarised and their punishment declared before the spotlight finally settles on the prophet's main subject: 'People of Israel. . . . Of all the nations on earth, you are the only one I have known and cared for. That is what makes your sins so terrible' (3:1, 2, all references from the *Good News Bible*).

In the chapters that follow, Amos has many harsh words for the rich merchants with their large and luxurious mansions, and for their womenfolk's dissolute, lazy lifestyle.

Amos exposes their ruthless exploitation of the poor. They 'sell into slavery honest men who cannot pay their debts . . . overcharge, use false measures, and tamper with the scales . . . sell worthless wheat at a high price' (2:6, 8:5, 6).

He also berates them for their corrupt religious practices and worthless ritual, and declares in the Lord's name: 'I hate your religious festivals. . . . When you bring me burnt-offerings and grain-offerings, I will not accept them. . . . Instead, let justice flow like a stream, and righteousness like a river' (5:21, 24).

Among a number of 'visions from the Lord' the prophet describes a wall against which the Lord holds a plumb-line – a simple plank with a cord attached and a weight on the end of it. Placed alongside the wall, it clearly shows the wall is out of line.

'My people are like a wall that is out of line. I will not change my mind again about punishing them' (7:8).

The last five verses of the book introduce a more optimistic note concerning the future rebuilding of those crooked walls. Did another writer add this passage to give a happy ending, as some scholars suggest?

We may never know, but we do know that it expresses an essential truth without which Amos's message is incomplete.

For alongside God's righteous judgement, his compassion and mercy remain, ensuring the possibility of forgiveness and restoration for all who turn to him.

OBADIAH

OBADIAH is the shortest book in the Old Testament – just 21 verses. The name means 'Servant of the Lord'. Several people in the Old Testament have this name, but none can be identified with this prophet, about whom nothing is known outside this book.

The prophecy is directed at the people of Edom, living to the south of the Dead Sea. The Edomites claimed Esau, Jacob's twin brother, as their ancestor. Indeed, Obadiah refers to them as 'descendants of Esau'.

You may recall the Genesis story (chapter 25) which tells how Jacob persuades his twin brother to sell him his birthright, ensuring that all the rights and privileges of the firstborn son pass from Esau to him.

The enmity this causes between the two brothers persists down the years, generating ill will between their descendants.

One illustration of this occurs during the second phase of the Israelites' long march to Canaan (Numbers 20).

The Israelites are following the route known as the 'King's Highway'. It passes through Edomite territory, and Moses's request to be allowed to travel through is refused, with the threat of armed resistance. A prolonged detour around the country is therefore necessary.

Much later, during King David's reign, Edom is conquered and Israelite troops are stationed there. Edom regains its independence during Solomon's reign, but its existence as a separate state remains precarious.

Obadiah's prophecy is prompted specifically by the conquest of Judah and Jerusalem by Nebuchadnezzar of Babylon in 587 BC.

The Edomites are accused of standing aside while Jerusalem's gates are broken down, of gloating over Judah's distress, of entering the beleaguered city and looting its riches, and even attempting to capture some of the escapees in order to turn them over to the enemy (verses 11-14).

We can understand the prophet's feelings, although history suggests there were faults on both sides.

It's wise to remember this is usually the case, not least in our own age, when in many parts of the world old feuds, often with small beginnings, are perpetuated and enlarged to engulf innocent people.

Obadiah would also have us remember, as he concludes his prophecy, that all nations are ultimately in the hands of God.

On what prophets call 'The day of the Lord', God will eventually ensure that right is vindicated and responsibility for wrongdoing – especially affecting the innocent – will be exposed and punished.

JONAH

THE Book of Jonah is not a record of prophecy. It's a tale about a prophet – and is one of the best known stories in the Old Testament, even if it's not always fully understood.

The dramatic tale begins with the hero, Jonah, being commanded by God to go and walk the streets of Nineveh, capital city of the hated Assyrian nation, and speak out against it.

Jonah refuses to do so – perhaps out of fear for his life, but more probably because he is afraid the Ninevites might respond to his message, repent of their evil deeds and be forgiven. After all the terrible suffering Assyria has inflicted on the Israelites, no self-respecting Jew would want to see *them* pardoned!

To avoid this hateful mission, Jonah flees in the opposite direction, boarding a ship bound for Spain.

On the high seas a violent storm develops. The distress of the superstitious sailors causes them to draw lots to discover who has angered the gods. Jonah's name comes up!

Jonah confesses that he is running away from a God-given task and tells the sailors to throw him overboard. They do so, and the sea is immediately calm.

A 'big fish' swallows Jonah alive. During the following three days and nights inside the fish Jonah has the opportunity to repent of his behaviour and offer a psalm of thanksgiving for his preservation. The fish then disgorges him on to a beach.

God again tells Jonah: 'Go to Nineveh and preach!'

This time Jonah obeys, whereupon the king, in sackcloth and ashes, orders his people to turn from their evil ways.

Is Jonah pleased? Not a bit! He is devastated. 'Now, Lord, let me die,' he says. 'I am better off dead than alive!'

In the final act of the drama Jonah goes outside the city, builds himself a rough shelter and waits to see what happens to Nineveh.

God causes a plant to grow overnight, giving Jonah protection. But in the morning the sun rises, the hot wind blows and the plant withers.

Jonah's anger towards God is silenced as God's voice is heard again: 'You're sorry for the loss of a single plant? What about *my* sorrow for the 120,000 children in this city who might be lost?'

And the lesson? There is no place in God's purposes for self-centred pride and feelings of superiority. Although Jonah belongs to God's chosen people, he must never forget that God cares for all races, even those who deny him and persecute his followers.

There's a supplementary word of encouragement, too. God gives Jonah a second chance to obey. The experience of many once-reluctant followers down the years is that God will always offer a second chance to those who sincerely regret their mistakes.

MICAH

WE know little about Micah as a person, but the time in which he lived can be established. He was a contemporary of Isaiah of Jerusalem. Unlike Isaiah, though, he did not live in the city but among the poor peasants in the southern countryside of Judah.

It's possible Micah lived through the time of the destruction of Samaria and Northern Israel (721 BC). Their fate seems imminent in the early chapters of the book.

But Micah's real interest is in Judah and its capital, Jerusalem. While Isaiah, the statesman-prophet, concerns himself with the activities of surrounding nations and the reaction of Judah's kings, Micah exposes the injustices inflicted on the poor by the rich upper class. 'When they want fields,' he writes, 'they seize them; when they want houses, they take them. No man's family or property is safe . . .' (2:2, 8, all references from the *Good News Bible*).

God has his say in similar vein: 'Men return from battle, thinking they are safe at home, but there you are, waiting to steal the coats off their backs. You drive the women of my people out of the homes they love, and you have robbed their children of my blessings for ever' (2:8, 9).

Elsewhere, Micah declares that bribery and corruption are rife among leaders, priests and false prophets alike, while the use of false weights and measures to defraud the poor is as widespread in Judah as Amos had earlier declared it to be in Israel.

The need for upright conduct is the real burden of Micah's message, which prompts his most memorable appeal: 'The Lord has told us what is good. What he requires of us is this: to do what is just, to show constant love, and to live in humble fellowship with our God' (6:8).

Micah's familiarity with the messages of Isaiah is illustrated by his often-declared faith in the survival of a believing remnant of Jews who would return from exile to Jerusalem.

Micah also reflects Isaiah's faith that a son of royal blood will be born to usher in a reign of safety and peace. He even names the birthplace as Bethlehem, a promise recalled by Matthew in his gospel hundreds of years later.

Notice, too, the vision, recorded by both prophets in identical words, of a time of future universal peace, when 'they will hammer their swords into ploughs and their spears into pruning-knives' (Isaiah 2:4, Micah 4:3).

We don't know what happened to Micah, but it seems his message lived on in the memory of the Jews. Years later a quotation from his prophecies helped save the life of Jeremiah at a critical moment in Judah's history (read the story in Jeremiah 26:10-24).

41

NAHUM

NOTHING is known about the prophet Nahum apart from what is recorded in the book named after him. Even the location of Elkosh, where he lived, cannot be identified with certainty.

Unlike other prophets, Nahum has words neither of reproof for Judah's sins nor of warning about the nation's coming judgement.

In fact Nahum has only one theme: the destruction of the city of Nineveh and the defeat of the Jewish people's long-time oppressor, Assyria – an event which eventually happens in 612 BC at the hands of the Median and Babylonian armies.

The name Nahum means 'comforter'. Presumably it was given to him because of the nature of his message to the people of Judah.

But is Nahum prophesying the coming fall of Assyria or writing about it afterwards? We cannot be sure. Future and past alternate as the story unfolds. It's possible the future tense is used to give dramatic effect to an account written soon after the event.

After an opening psalm describing God's power and intention to destroy all who frustrate his will, Nahum introduces his theme by announcing the arrival of a messenger bearing news of victory.

Then, in chapter 2, the prophet launches into a dramatic poem which describes in graphic detail the siege and overthrow of Nineveh, the great capital city of the Assyrians.

All the ingredients are there: the menacing troops in their red tunics, bearing red shields; the chariot horses restlessly prancing, waiting for the signal to attack; the battering-ram in place.

Then the city gates burst open and the soldiers pour through, killing, taking prisoners and plundering the city's treasures.

A second poem, in chapter 3, adds further lurid details of the fighting in the city. Men stumble over piles of bodies. It is a picture of utter destruction.

The prophecy ends with a kind of elegy in prose. Nahum compares Nineveh's destruction with that of Thebes, ancient capital of Egypt, some 50 years earlier.

In the heyday of their power the Assyrians had spread across the Fertile Crescent like swarms of locusts, devouring and destroying wherever they went. But now those swarms have gone and the silence of death is everywhere.

Did Nahum live to see the next 25 years, when Judah refused to change its ways and was itself overthrown by the Babylonian conquerors of Assyria?

We don't know. Nahum's book ends on a note of triumph. Any thought that Nahum might be appalled by the wanton destruction of Nineveh is dispelled in the final verse: 'All those who hear the news of your destruction clap their hands for joy' (3:19, *Good News Bible*).

HABAKKUK

ON our sometimes difficult journey of exploration through the messages of the minor prophets we now meet Habakkuk – a man not afraid to question God's actions.

Like many of us, Habakkuk is disturbed by man's inhumanity to man. He protests to God: 'How can you endure to look on such wrongdoing? Destruction and violence are all round me, and there is fighting and quarrelling everywhere' (1:3, all quotations from the *Good News Bible*).

The first answer Habakkuk receives is that God knows what he is doing in using a powerful army to discipline his backsliding people. But the prophet is not satisfied, repeating his complaint with greater intensity: 'Lord . . . , you are my God, holy and eternal . . . how can you stand these treacherous, evil men? . . . why are you silent while they destroy people who are more righteous than they are?' (1:12, 13).

Chapter 2 describes how, in his perplexity, Habakkuk resolves to wait for a while and watch events in the hope of receiving further guidance.

Eventually the prophet is reassured, delivering a prophecy foretelling the ultimate destruction of his country's invaders.

At one point Habakkuk pauses to declare: 'The earth will be as full of the knowledge of the Lord's glory as the seas are full of water' (2:14). Centuries later those words inspired a hymn popular in many churches today:

> *Nearer and nearer draws the time,*
>   *The time that shall surely be*
> *When the earth shall be filled with the glory of God*
>   *As the waters cover the sea.*

Such confidence inspires the prophet in chapter 3 to compose a prayer, or psalm, extolling the greatness of God who rules heaven and earth alike, destroying his enemies and rescuing his people.

So to the final prayer, one of the Old Testament's great affirmations of faith which triumphs in adversity – faith that God's victory, however long delayed, will nevertheless come.

On such a foundation of trust and confidence, all who believe in God may experience an abiding sense of peace and joy.

ZEPHANIAH

A BOOK of 'almost unrelieved gloom' is how one commentary describes Zephaniah. It will be helpful therefore to explore a little of the life and times of the prophet to try to discover the reason for the tone of his message.

We are told at the beginning that Zephaniah is a descendant of the good King Hezekiah – probably his great-great-grandson.

Hezekiah worked long and hard to reform his nation, restoring the Temple, re-commencing its services, and seeking to cleanse it from idolatrous worship.

But Hezekiah's son Manasseh, who succeeded him, reversed all his father's religious policies, and introduced idol worship, including child sacrifice. He even erected a heathen image in the Temple itself.

When Manasseh's 55-year reign ended, his son Amon followed in his footsteps. But, just two years later, he was assassinated, and his son Josiah became king, at the age of eight. Nothing is known about the first 10 years of his reign.

One imagines the young Zephaniah growing up during that time of great uncertainty, his family constantly recounting the achievements of his ancestor-king and the disasters that followed. Against such a background, the prophet's gloomy predictions are understandable.

That Zephaniah was a city man is clear from his vivid descriptions of Jerusalem, and his exposure of the various forms of idolatry being practised there.

Indeed he seems, from these early predictions, to believe that nothing less than the complete destruction of the city can be expected. Later, however, he softens his condemnation a little, declaring that 'the Lord is still in the city' (3:5, *Good News Bible*).

From that point on, Zephaniah's message contains elements of hope for the future. In words already familiar from our reading of Habakkuk's prophecy, Zephaniah advises his people to wait until God's time arrives to punish evil nations and exalt his 'humble and lowly people' who have remained faithful.

Zephaniah delivers a prophetic survey and judgement on surrounding nations – Philistia in the west, Moab and Ammon to the east, Ethiopia in the south, and the arch-enemy Assyria to the north – reminding the people of God's sovereignty over the whole world.

The final seven verses of Zephaniah are described in the *Good News Bible* as 'A Song of Joy'. In them he forecasts the final overthrow of Judah's enemies, the return of the exiles, and the re-establishment of Jerusalem. The theme and atmosphere are reminiscent of truths given fuller expression in the second part of the Book of Isaiah.

HAGGAI

HAGGAI and the other two remaining Old Testament prophecies belong to the period during which groups of Jews return from exile in Babylon to their homeland.

This becomes possible because of the enlightened policy of King Cyrus of Persia who, after conquering Babylon, issues a decree permitting captive people to return home if they wish. Many Jews do so, though others remain in their adopted land.

One of the first tasks on arriving home is to build an altar for the recommencement of sacrifices. A start is then made on rebuilding the Temple.

Regretfully, local opposition leads to this being abandoned for some 18 years until, largely due to the encouragement of the prophets Haggai and Zechariah, the work recommences and is eventually completed. The story is told in the Book of Ezra.

Haggai's messages are practical and down-to-earth. He chides the people for giving priority to their own well-built houses while God's house lies in ruins.

He draws attention to the poor harvests gleaned from drought-ridden fields, resulting in pitifully low wages for labourers. To quote the King James version, it is like putting their wages into a bag with holes! (Do I hear someone say times haven't changed much?)

Eventually the prophet's message is heeded and, led by Zerubbabel the Governor and Joshua the High Priest, the work begins once more.

But people sometimes need a lot of encouragement and, as chapter 2 indicates, the workers become smitten with the 'good old days' syndrome!

They reflect on the splendour of the old Temple built by King Solomon and cannot believe that such grandeur can be repeated. (But, one wonders, how many of them would even have seen that grand edifice, destroyed 60 years earlier?)

Haggai persists with his message: 'Don't be discouraged . . . I am with you . . . the new Temple will be more splendid than the old one, and . . . I will give my people prosperity and peace' (2:4, 9, *Good News Bible*).

A curious conversation is recorded between the prophet and some priests concerning ancient regulations governing ritual defilement. The reason for the conversation is not clear. Perhaps the labourers working on the holy site needed guidance.

Resuming his theme, Haggai gives renewed assurance that, as a sign of God's blessing, bountiful harvests will follow completion of the Temple.

ZECHARIAH

THE name Zechariah is common in Scripture. Almost 30 people in the Old Testament have this name. The Book of Zechariah is one of the longest of the minor prophets and is somewhat complex. Many students believe Zechariah is responsible for only the first eight chapters, the remaining six having been added anonymously.

As mentioned in the study of the Book of Haggai, Zechariah shares with Haggai the task of encouraging the returned Jewish exiles to recommence and complete the work of rebuilding Jerusalem's ruined Temple.

But Zechariah has wider interests – for example, emphasising and expanding the belief that Zerubbabel the Governor and Joshua the High Priest are the ordained leaders of state and church in the renewed community.

In one of his eight visions, Zechariah pictures the ceremonial cleansing of the high priest for his important ministry.

An earlier vision portrays a workman carrying a line for measuring the boundaries of Jerusalem. Two heavenly beings confront him and declare that the city will grow beyond the possibility of human measurement, the Lord himself becoming a 'wall of fire' to protect it.

This hopeful and encouraging message emerges at various points in Zechariah's writings and is the theme of his final prophecy, in which he describes the Jews' future influence on 'many peoples and powerful nations' who will have heard that God is with them (8:22, *Good News Bible*).

Chapters 9 to 14 introduce a different type of prophecy which looks into the far future and, through visions and cryptic sayings, proclaims the final overthrow of evil and the triumphant fulfilment of God's ultimate purpose for his creation.

Few of its details are meant to be taken literally. Indeed, scholarly help is needed to interpret what is known as 'apocalyptic' prophecy.

However, two quotations from this part of the book find their way into the gospel story. In verses 9 and 10 of chapter 9 we read of the future Messianic king riding into Jerusalem on the back of a donkey to offer peace to the nations. Jesus deliberately chose to enter Jerusalem in this way on the day we celebrate as Palm Sunday.

Then in the account of Christ's crucifixion, the apostle John, watching a soldier thrust a spear into the lifeless body of Jesus, quotes a phrase from Zechariah: 'They shall look on . . . him whom they have pierced' (12:10, *New English Bible*).

Turn finally from much that is hard to understand to a simple, moving statement in the last two verses of the book which outline the kind of life God expects of his children. Their worship, work and home life – represented by 'bowls before the altar' (*NEB*), 'the harness bells of the horses' (*GNB*) and 'every cooking pot in Jerusalem and in all Judah' (*GNB*) – will bear the motto: 'Dedicated to the Lord'.

Challenging? Yes, indeed! But should any part of life be excluded from him who is the Lord of life?

MALACHI

IN Malachi, the final book of Old Testament prophecy, we remain in the period following the Jews' return from exile.

Judging from his subject matter, Malachi (whose name means 'my messenger') is active some time later than Haggai and Zechariah – perhaps during the next generation.

By Malachi's time, the Temple has been rebuilt and its services established. But the Jewish people have become apathetic. They are drifting into a dangerous disregard for some of the law's requirements.

The fact that Malachi is writing his message down suggests he is facing resistance and needs to argue his case in response to questions from the people. There is an illustration of this at the very beginning of the book. In response to the Lord's claim 'I have always loved you' the Jews ask, 'How have you shown your love for us?' The prophet's answer then follows (1:2, all references from the *Good News Bible*).

There are six examples of this question-and-answer style in the book. And the subjects? To begin with, and at some length, the priests are condemned for dishonouring God by offering blind, sick or lame animals on the altar. This is in direct contravention of covenant law (see Deuteronomy 15:21). 'Try giving an animal like that to the governor!' exclaims the prophet (1:8).

Next, Malachi turns to a problem which had earlier caused Ezra such distress – that of marriage between Jewish men and foreign women.

An even more serious threat to the Jewish way of life is the fact that some men are divorcing 'the wife you married when you were young' in order to marry attractive young foreigners (2:14).

'I hate divorce . . . I hate it when one of you does such a cruel thing to his wife,' is God's judgement through Malachi (2:16).

A further complaint relates to the law on tithing. Malachi issues the challenge: 'Bring the full amount of your tithes . . . and . . . I will . . . pour out on you in abundance all kinds of good things' (3:10).

As always, however, there are people who remain true to God despite every temptation. For them Malachi has a gracious word (see 3:16-18 and 4:2, 3). The children's hymn 'When he cometh . . . to make up his jewels' is based on one of these verses.

Finally, Malachi links the Old Testament to the New with his promise of a special messenger who will prepare the way for the Lord, who will 'suddenly come to his Temple' (3:1).

At the very end of the book, Malachi names this messenger 'Elijah' – meaning that his personality and message would remind people of that great prophet from an earlier time.

Gospel writers have no doubt that John the Baptist's appearance fulfils this promise (see Matthew 11:14).

49

BETWEEN THE TESTAMENTS

'BETWEEN the testaments' is the title sometimes used to describe the period of some four centuries between the Jews' return to Israel after their captivity in Babylon and the birth of Jesus Christ.

During the early part of this period, Greek influence is growing. Under Alexander the Great it spreads throughout the Mediterranean region. The Jews preserve a measure of independence by ingratiating themselves with the Greek leadership.

When Alexander dies in 323 BC, his empire is divided among his generals and Judaea once more becomes the arena for a struggle between two powers centred on Egypt and Syria.

Eventually a Syrian ruler, Antiochus IV, tries to impose the Greek way of life on the Jews. Many Jews resist, rise up in revolt, win their independence and expand their territory. (This so-called Maccabean period was referred to when we studied the Book of Daniel.)

Though the Greek Empire passes away, its language remains and becomes the medium of communication throughout its former territories. In due time, the Greek language is an important aid to the spreading of the Christian gospel.

Rome becomes the dominant power during the final century of this period.

In 63 BC, Judaea finally loses its independence when a Roman army under Pompey invades Palestine to put an end to rivalry and conflict between Jewish leaders.

As the Roman Empire expands, a vast network of roads is built. This enables its armies to move easily to distant parts, maintaining what is known as 'The Roman Peace'. Along these roads, Christian disciples are later able to travel in safety, carrying the gospel message.

Another development is the establishment and growth of Jewish settlements in many of the larger cities. They are known as 'The Jews of the Dispersion' or 'The Diaspora'. When Paul and other apostles set out to carry their message they go first to these Jewish communities, assured at least of a hearing, even if the reception is mixed.

Greek language, Roman roads, scattered Jewish communities – each contributes to the spread of the gospel of God's undying love as revealed in Jesus, to whose story we turn next.

INTRODUCTION TO THE GOSPELS

FOLLOWING the events which took place on the Day of Pentecost and its immediate aftermath, we read: 'And every day in the Temple and in people's homes they (the apostles) continued to teach and preach the Good News about Jesus the Messiah' (Acts 5:42, *Good News Bible*).

Thus it was by word of mouth that the story of the earthly life and ministry of Jesus Christ was first made known. Stories of healing miracles, down-to-earth parables, teaching about the Kingdom of God, and so on, were eagerly listened to, remembered and treasured within the many groups of Christians which began to spring up throughout Palestine and beyond.

Some of the more moving details of Jesus' ministry would be repeated again and again, perhaps especially the dramatic events of the final, so-called Passion week, which, when the Gospels came to be written, occupied almost one-third of each of them.

In the excitement of those early days, Christians were no doubt adequately served by this constant re-telling of remembered events, so that for a period of about 30 years little, if anything, was written down. However, as converts multiplied and centres increased, the number of apostles and eye-witnesses, depleted through old age and death, could not cope with the need for instruction. A written record thus became an urgent requirement.

In addition, the event called 'the second coming of Jesus', which was keenly anticipated and thought to be imminent, did not take place in those early years, so that written guidance was needed to enable Christians to cope with the turbulent world around them.

Many scholars accept that the first Gospel to be written was by John Mark. Some time after being with Paul during his first journey, Mark went to Rome (see 1 Peter 5:13). There he listened closely to the preaching of Peter and, following the latter's martyrdom in about 65 AD, wrote his Gospel, basing it largely on Peter's recollections.

Both Matthew and Luke in turn used parts of Mark's account, adjusting and combining them with information each had gathered from elsewhere. The similarity thus achieved by these three writers led scholars to refer to them as 'synoptic' gospels, meaning they could be 'viewed together'. However, as readers soon discover, the Gospel of John, written perhaps towards the close of the first century, is very different.

In today's world of mass media information, we know that two or more accounts of the same story can differ on details. It is important to remember this as the Gospels are compared. The remarkable fact is that through each of these varied portraits we meet the same Jesus: for Mark, the man of action and authority; for Matthew, the promised

Messiah and teacher; for Luke, the incomparable story-teller and compassionate healer; for John, the divine Son and very Word of God.

Taken together, they present a vivid and living portrait of the Saviour who 'came to seek and to save the lost' and to be the ever-present companion for all who believe and trust in him.

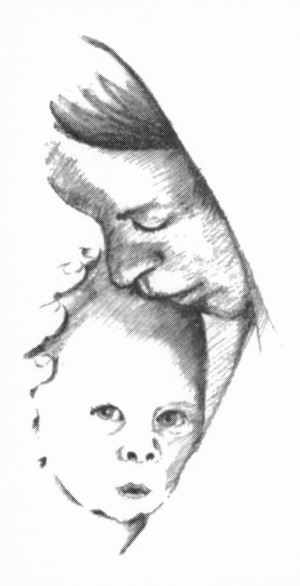

MATTHEW

ALTHOUGH Mark's Gospel was the first to be written, Matthew's Gospel appropriately precedes it in the Bible, providing as it does a firm link with Old Testament prophecies.

Many quotations stress the claim that what God promises through the words of various prophets he now fulfils in the life and ministry of Jesus. Matthew's appeal to Jews is to recognise that the promised Messiah has now appeared, and to receive him.

The Gospel begins with a genealogy of Jesus, tracing his ancestry through three sets of 14 generations through King David and right back to Abraham.

A second feature of appeal to Jews is that Mark's and Luke's phrase 'Kingdom of God' is replaced in Matthew's Gospel by 'Kingdom of Heaven'. This reflects the Jews' hesitancy to use the sacred name of God.

Another sign of the Jewish appeal of this Gospel is that the teaching of Jesus is presented in five segments, the longest and best-known of which is the 'sermon on the mount' (recorded in chapters five to seven).

These teaching passages may have been deliberately arranged as if to form a 'new law' to supersede the old, as contained in the first five books of the Old Testament. Each of the five teaching segments can be identified by noting a common phrase at the end: 'When Jesus finished saying these things ...' (*Good News Bible*, for example 7:28).

Matthew was a tax-collector at the time he was called by Jesus to be a disciple. In two other Gospels he is called Levi. Little more is known about him.

Some scholars have wondered, for various reasons, whether Matthew wrote the whole of his book in its final form, but there is general agreement that the collection of Jesus' teaching is his. This alone is sufficient reason to link Matthew's name with the Gospel.

Following the genealogy, Matthew's prologue continues with the announcement to Mary of the coming birth of Jesus, the visit of astrologers who followed a star to find and worship the infant, and the flight of the young family to Egypt to escape the wrath of Herod and the return to Nazareth. After that, the pattern of events follows the order in Mark's Gospel, with the books of teaching appropriately inserted and with some editorial revision.

The teaching sections provide this Gospel's outstanding contribution to our knowledge of Jesus' earthly ministry.

As we read the sermon on the mount we note Jesus' support for the ancient Jewish law, but with his vital emphasis on the need for right inner motivation, with spirit, thought and action unified in pursuit of worthy living.

To absorb such teaching and weave it into our lifestyle will prove for us the truth of Jesus' claim that a 'house' built on such foundations will stand up to life's severest storms. And let's remember this Gospel's closing promise to the disciples, and surely to every believer: 'I will be with you always, to the end of the age' (28:20, *GNB*).

MARK

MARK'S Gospel is the shortest. More importantly, it was the first to be written, perhaps as early as 68 AD. Also, both Matthew and Luke use some of Mark's book when compiling their own. Mark's Gospel is therefore particularly authoritative.

Who is Mark? Almost certainly he is the John Mark mentioned in Acts 12:12. It is in his mother's house that the first Christians meet. Later, Mark becomes Paul's companion on his first missionary journey.

Mark probably includes a reference to himself in his Gospel. Many believe he is the young man who follows Jesus and the disciples from the house where they celebrate the 'last supper' to the Garden of Gethsemane, and is almost arrested as Jesus is led away (see 14:51).

Some years later, Mark becomes a companion to Peter, from whom – according to an early Christian writer named Papias – Mark gleans much of the material for his Gospel.

Mark presents Jesus as a man of action and authority. A word which appears constantly in his book is translated in English versions as 'immediately', 'straightway' or 'at once'. Jesus' response to human need, and people's response to him, is immediate.

Mark includes few long passages of Christ's teaching, but graphically reports many of his miracles – demonstrations of Jesus' power over nature, sickness and evil spirits.

Following a brief introduction about the preaching and baptising of John the Baptist, Mark's early chapters focus on Jesus' ministry in the area around the Sea of Galilee. Here, large crowds follow Jesus, and the first disciples are recruited.

Read about 'a day in the life of Jesus' in chapter 1:21-34. Note some rumblings of early opposition in chapter 2, a selection of miracles in chapter 3 and of parables in chapter 4.

A crucial point is reached at a place called Caesarea Philippi (8:27-30). Here Jesus questions his disciples: 'Who do men say . . . who do you say . . . that I am?' From this point on, while opposition increases, Jesus – with face turned steadfastly towards Jerusalem – tries to prepare his disciples for his coming suffering and death.

The last six chapters portray the events of 'holy week', from the entry into Jerusalem on Palm Sunday to Jesus' death and resurrection. The happenings are remembered so vividly by this youthful eyewitness that the Church has largely adopted his order of events in its celebrations ever since.

In the earliest surviving manuscripts, Mark's Gospel ends at 16:8, but the *Good News Bible* includes two alternative endings which appear in other manuscripts.

How did Mark intend to end his story? Was his original last page lost? We may never know.

LUKE

LUKE – described as 'an educated Gentile and a doctor' – is the only Gospel writer who was not a Jew. His Gospel is volume one of a two-part work, the second volume being the Acts of the Apostles.

A glance at the opening verses of each confirms this. Luke did not witness the gospel events in Palestine but studied documents which were already circulating, so as to provide Theophilus with as reliable a record as possible.

We do not know how or when Luke became a Christian, but we know he joined Paul as a companion during Paul's second missionary journey. Among the documents Luke studied was Mark's Gospel. Clearly, Luke also studied the separate record of Jesus' teaching, now lost, referred to in a previous chapter.

Also, much additional information may have been gathered in Palestine during Paul's two-year imprisonment in Caesarea.

Some of this relates to the birth and childhood of Jesus, and includes some details as to the birth of John the Baptist. To the well-known stories relating to the birth of Jesus is added the only known incident from Jesus' childhood when, at the age of 12, with his parents, he visited Jerusalem and its Temple.

As Luke begins to recount the story of Christ's ministry, he slots in his own 'genealogy' of Jesus, as Matthew does in his Gospel. Luke, however, traces Jesus' ancestry, through Joseph, right back to Adam and to God. The pen-portrait of Jesus painted by Luke is of a man of prayer, seeking his heavenly Father's guidance in all major decisions and teaching his followers the worth of such communion.

Here is the Christ of large and tender sympathy for the poor and outcast, also of reverent tenderness towards the many women who figure in the story.

Luke's considerable artistry with words heightens the impact of some of Jesus' most memorable stories, such as the Prodigal Son and the Good Samaritan. This same ability produces perhaps the loveliest story of them all, of two sad disciples journeying home to Emmaus on the evening of the day of Jesus' Resurrection, and of their joy at meeting the risen Lord.

The Gospel of Luke is supremely a gospel of joy. It begins with four early songs of praise which are woven into the first two chapters (identified in the *Good News Bible* translation by being set in poetic format). It ends as the disciples leave the place of the Ascension and return to Jerusalem 'filled with great joy' to await the promised Holy Spirit.

The French historian Ernest Renan is often quoted for his comment that Luke's Gospel is 'the most beautiful book we possess'. High praise indeed!

JOHN

THE three Gospels so far studied – Matthew, Mark and Luke – have much in common. Sources of information and the recorded pattern of events, for example. John's Gospel is different.

There are no stories here of the birth and childhood of Jesus. Instead there is a prologue proclaiming God as the eternal Word who 'became a human being and . . . lived among us' (1:14, all references from the *Good News Bible*).

Then John the Baptist is introduced, he in turn presenting Jesus as 'the Lamb of God, who takes away the sin of the world!' (1:29).

Many features distinguish the Gospel of John. As described in the first three Gospels, Jesus' earthly ministry could have been accomplished within a year. But John speaks of at least three visits to Jerusalem at certain festival times, which would require three years.

However, it is to the accounts of Jesus' teaching that John contributes so much that is unique.

Long discourses arise out of several miracles, presented as 'signs' of Jesus' power and authority. Word-pictures abound describing the nature of Jesus' claims, such as 'I am the bread of life . . . I am the light of the world . . . I am the good shepherd.'

The name of John, son of Zebedee, is rightly linked to this Gospel, but the possibility that it was actually compiled by someone else is suggested by the use of the phrase 'that other disciple, whom Jesus loved' instead of the name John (21:20).

Note also the reference in 21:24: 'He is the disciple who spoke of these things, the one who also wrote them down; and we know that what he said is true.'

Early documents suggest that a second John, known as 'The Elder', compiled the Gospel from the aged disciple's personal memories.

John contributes much new information and insight concerning the closing week of Jesus' earthly life. In place of the other Gospels' account of the 'Last Supper' John describes a similar event at which Jesus washes the disciples' feet and prepares them for the difficult days ahead with much teaching and a moving final prayer.

A final bonus, following the crucifixion and Resurrection, is the Gospel's closing chapter, with its lovely account of a lakeside breakfast and the brief conversation with Peter intimating Peter's forgiveness and restoration to leadership.

The deeply spiritual message of John's Gospel is presented with a simplicity of language which makes it one of the richest treasures of biblical revelation.

ACTS OF THE APOSTLES

THE Acts of the Apostles – the unique document recording the birth, dynamic growth and development of the Christian Church during its first 35 years – is Luke's second volume. The first, as we have already noted, is the Gospel which bears his name.

Theophilus, for whom both volumes are written, is probably an important Gentile who has become a Christian.

Acts begins with the only detailed accounts we have of the Ascension of Jesus and the choice of a successor to Judas the betrayer.

Then we have Luke's description of the dramatic bestowal of the Holy Spirit on the disciples, marking the Church's establishment in the world. Taking this as his theme, Luke identifies the Spirit as the true motivator of Christian activity, guiding the early believers where to go or not to go, and giving them courage in adversity and the strength to endure.

Two names are prominent. The first is Peter, leader of the disciples and the first to welcome Gentiles (non-Jews) into their fellowship.

Then Paul, transformed from arch-persecutor to dynamic missionary leader through a dramatic conversion, takes centre stage. His three remarkable missionary journeys help the Christian message spread through Asia Minor and into Europe, with churches being established in many towns.

Where does Luke's information come from? His personal interest in Antioch, the first Gentile church (indicated in chapters 11 and 13), suggests he may have lived there for a time. But he later joins Paul's party on its second journey (note the change from 'they' to 'we' in 16:6-10) and is an eyewitness to the remaining events he describes.

Luke's special skill in story-telling (seen in his Gospel) is amply illustrated again in Acts, nowhere more memorably than in his account of the voyage of Paul and his party to Rome (chapter 27).

Luke's record concludes with a picture of Paul settled in his own hired house in Rome, welcoming visitors and free to proclaim his message. But it sounds more like a pause than the end of the story, and indeed it is!

For although the early disciples die, their message continues. Others take up the mission and the Church continues to spread throughout the world. As the Jewish scholar Gamaliel says to a worried Jewish Council: '. . . do not take any action against these men. Leave them alone! If what they have planned and done is of human origin, it will disappear, but if it comes from God, you cannot possibly defeat them' (5:38, 39, *Good News Bible*).

It was from God. The first Christians were not defeated and their successors in every age, including our own, continue to share their victory.

INTRODUCTION TO THE LETTERS OF PAUL

THE New Testament presents a more detailed picture of Paul's contribution to the Christian Church than of any other leader. Even Peter, rightly prominent in the very beginning, takes second place in terms of information behind this 'Apostle to the Gentiles'.

There are two obvious reasons for this. Firstly that Luke, author of the Acts of the Apostles – the only biblical history of the first 30 or so Christian years – became a companion of Paul. He records, sometimes as an eyewitness, the story of those fascinating journeys and many other events in which the apostle was involved. The other reason is that the 13 letters Paul wrote during his ministry fill in much additional detail about people and places, as well as providing much information about the preaching and teaching in the early Church. Most, if not all of these letters were written and circulated in the Church before the first written Gospel appeared.

Paul invariably dictated his letters to an assistant (see Romans 16:22), but sometimes added a sentence or two at the end in his own handwriting, perhaps to confirm the genuineness of the letter. According to Galatians 6:11, he wrote in 'large letters', which suggests he may have suffered from poor eyesight. On completion, each letter was entrusted to one of his helpers who carried and safely delivered it to its destination. Letters were sometimes passed round for other church groups to read, as referred to in the final verses of the Colossian letter.

The earliest letters were probably written to the Thessalonian church, established during Paul's second missionary journey, though some scholars wonder if Galatians should be considered the first. This keenly argued debate can be read in the commentaries for those who are interested.

These were days of the Church's early growth, when questions arose requiring urgent and authoritative answers which Paul and the other letter-writers sought to supply. The process can be clearly seen in the first letter to the Corinthians, where both verbal and written queries are itemised and dealt with one by one. In the excitement and enthusiasm of those days there were men who moved in among the new converts, spreading false teaching. Paul laboured to expose them in strong, passionate language, determined that the purity of the fledgling Christian faith must be maintained.

While much of Paul's writing breathes an air of intense activity, there are letters which reflect a calmer atmosphere, with less tension and quiet confidence. The so-called 'prison letters', – Ephesians, Philippians, Colossians and Philemon – are examples. One letter above all, that to the Roman church, shows extra care in construction and maturity of thought. Paul writes it in preparation for an intended visit to Rome, from where he hoped to set out for 'more worlds to conquer' for Christ. This summary of his personal faith, hammered out during the strains and stresses of many miles and long years in the service of Christ, has been called by one commentator 'the most profound work ever written'.

The man portrayed in these letters is totally committed to the Christ he met on the Damascus road. We sense his wonder that he, an educated Pharisee and one-time persecutor of Christians, is God's chosen instrument on behalf of all who are not of the Jewish race. Strong convictions give his writings an air of authority. He cares deeply for the whole Christian family, though at times impatient with human weakness and angry towards all who seek to falsify the gospel message. Subjected to much suffering and persecution, he bears it with dignity, assured of the sufficiency of God's grace. Paul leaves a precious legacy of truth which, under the Holy Spirit's guidance, will enhance the understanding of all who seek the highest and best in Christian life and experience.

ROMANS

CENTURIES before the invention of such things as telephones and typewriters, handwritten letters enabled the leaders of the Christian Church to keep in touch with their expanding fellowship of believers.

Thirteen of the New Testament letters are attributed to Paul, who usually dictated them to a colleague. They are not in chronological order. Romans, written at Corinth towards the close of Paul's third missionary journey, is probably placed first because it contains his most complete presentation of the gospel. Indeed, it has been sub-titled 'the gospel according to Paul'.

Begin by reading chapter 15:22-33, in which Paul explains why he is writing – namely to prepare for his hoped-for visit to Rome. His vision is still to expand the frontiers of the Kingdom of Christ, perhaps as far as Spain.

The letter is long and complex, but is easier to follow when considered in four parts, each dealing with one aspect of the overall theme: God's great plan of salvation through the redeeming work of Christ.

Part One (chapters 1-4): This could be headed 'What Christ has done FOR us'. After a short introduction Paul exposes at length the sinfulness of human nature, in Jews as well as Gentiles.

God's purpose is to save them, as summarised in 3:23, 24. But this salvation will be received only by the exercise of faith. To illustrate this Paul uses the story of Abraham, who 'believed God, and . . . God accepted him as righteous' (4:3, *Good News Bible*).

Part Two (chapters 5-8): This could be headed 'What Christ does WITHIN us'. The great change brought about through Christ in the power of the Holy Spirit is likened to a kind of death to sin and resurrection to new life, or like liberation from slavery to serve Christ freely.

From a life of struggle and failure we can emerge to enjoy victorious living, and know with assurance that nothing can separate us from the love of Christ.

Part Three (chapters 9-11): Paul leaves the main theme for a while to ponder why the majority of Jews – 'my own race' – have rejected Jesus as the promised Messiah.

Paul uses many quotations from the Old Testament to show how God's purpose for the Jews was constantly frustrated by their unbelief and disobedience. But he is glad that many Gentiles have become believers and expresses his confidence that one day the Jews will be brought back into the Kingdom.

Part Four (chapters 12-15): This could be headed 'What Christ wants to do THROUGH us'. Consecrated to the service of Christ, the Christian uses every gift for the benefit of all within the fellowship, showing Christlike love and tolerance when disagreements arise and special concern for those weaker in the faith. Beyond the fellowship there are duties to fulfil towards the state, and right conduct to display at all times.

The letter ends, as letters often do, with greetings from Paul and others who are with him to their friends.

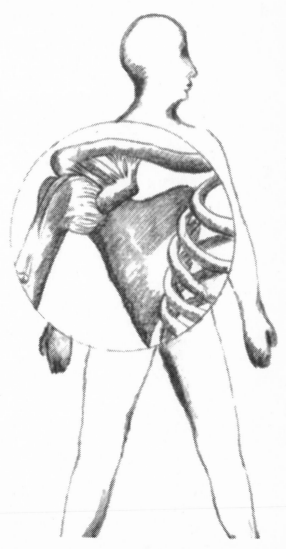

FIRST LETTER TO THE CORINTHIANS

CORINTH, in New Testament times, was a large commercial city on the narrow isthmus to the south of Greece, where people of many races and religions intermingled. Its name had become a byword for low moral standards. The beginnings of the Christian Church there are described in the 18th chapter of the Acts of the Apostles. At the time of writing his letters to that church, Paul had visited the city once and would visit it twice more.

As you read these chapters, try to imagine an entirely new Christian church in a largely pagan environment, facing many challenges and working out, with the help of Paul and other leaders, how to behave as members of this new community. For example, they must maintain their unity and not yield to pressure to favour one Christian leader more than others (chapters 1-4). Any deviation from high moral conduct must be severely dealt with.

Paul gives an instance of a serious case needing prompt attention (5:9). As Christians they should not take one another to court to resolve disputes (chapter 6). If they cannot settle things within the fellowship they should put up with the situation.

These problems are raised by 'some people of Chloe's family' who visit Paul and share their concerns with him.

But the local leaders in Corinth are themselves worried about various matters, and write to Paul, who comments on these from chapter seven onwards.

Marital relationships are posing problems, as they often do today. Paul's guidance may sound strange to modern ears, but note the strong expectation of Christ's early return to earth (7:29-31). In such a context his advice that 'each one should remain . . . in the same condition as he was when he was called' (verse 24, *Good News Bible*) is understandable.

Read carefully the comments in chapter 8 on shopping in the market place where meat which had been offered at heathen altars might be on sale. Obviously, idols had no power to contaminate meat so it should be all right to purchase it. But, says Paul, if such action disturbed a new convert then the meat should not be bought. No action should be undertaken which might lead a weaker person to stumble (verses 9-13).

Guidance concerning 'gifts of the Holy Spirit' (chapters 12-14) includes perhaps Paul's most memorable passage where he describes the greatest gift of all, Christian love (chapter 13). Chapter 15 is probably the earliest account to be written on the subject of the Resurrection of Christ and of all believers. These words have brought comfort and peace to Christians everywhere through the centuries.

Note that Paul personally signs this letter, guaranteeing its genuineness.

SECOND LETTER TO THE CORINTHIANS

AS we begin to read Paul's second letter to the Christians at Corinth, it becomes clear that relations between Paul and that church have deteriorated since the first letter was sent.

From various references it seems that the wrongs exposed in the first letter have not been dealt with. There are also false apostles whose aim is to discredit Paul and refute his claim to be an apostle.

In chapter 2 Paul alludes to a visit he made to Corinth which caused sadness among the Christians there.

He followed his visit with a letter, no copy of which has survived. But from chapter 7 of what is known as Paul's second letter to the Corinthians (really his third) we learn that this so-called 'severe letter' was carried to Corinth by Titus, one of Paul's trusted helpers.

After waiting for some time at Ephesus, Paul sets out for Macedonia, where he meets Titus on his way back from Corinth. From him Paul learns, with great joy, that both message and messenger were well received and the matters dealt with satisfactorily.

Earlier in the letter (chapters 3-6), Paul writes at length, and with deep feeling, about the ministry with which God has entrusted him.

Paul sees himself as a common clay pot through which God's light is shining. In his preaching he is not commending himself but Jesus.

Though this ministry causes Paul much suffering, his spirit is renewed while he keeps his eyes fixed on eternal things. The reminder that life's true goal is God gives him the courage to keep going.

Later, in chapters 8 and 9, Paul returns to the subject of the collection of money for the Judaean Christians, which was briefly mentioned in the first letter. He now urges them to follow the example of Christ and respond as generously as other churches have. The Corinthians should bear in mind that 'God loves the one who gives gladly' (9:7, *Good News Bible*).

The remaining chapters (10-13) reveal Paul in a very different mood. Responding defensively to criticism, he vigorously asserts his apostolic claim, reminding his readers that he, and not the detractors, had first preached the gospel to them.

Paul responds to the boasting of the false apostles by some 'boasting' of his own, quoting an impressive list of sufferings he has endured for Christ's sake.

Paul had indeed been granted a special spiritual revelation from God, but it was through a persistent physical ailment that he had learned that God's grace would always sustain him. Finally Paul calls on the Corinthians to examine their own hearts and mend their ways, before concluding with a well-known benediction.

Are these last four chapters part of the 'severe' letter referred to earlier? Some commentators believe so.

GALATIANS

GALATIA was a Roman province in Asia Minor where, on his first missionary journey, Paul established churches at Iconium, Lystra, Derbe and Pisidian Antioch (see Acts 13 and 14).

Paul has just arrived back at his home base of Syrian Antioch when disturbing news reaches him. Some Jewish Christians are moving among the new Galatian congregations claiming that Gentile members must adopt the Jewish practice of circumcision and observe the Law of Moses.

Paul responds by writing this letter. Understandably, he is furious. After the briefest of greetings, he protests that this new teaching formed no part of his message to them.

Paul testifies that both his conversion and his call to preach the gospel to Gentiles were by direct revelation from God. The apostles – Peter, whom he met three years after his conversion, and the others, whom he did not meet for a further 14 years – seem to have approved his special ministry to Gentiles.

However, Paul does mention an unfortunate incident which seems to show Peter's inconsistency. When visiting Antioch, Peter associated and ate with Gentile Christians until a party of Jews arrived from Jerusalem, whereupon Peter withdrew from Gentile company.

Paul now launches into a vigorous defence of his own position, namely that salvation is received solely through faith in Jesus Christ, and not by circumcision or slavish obedience to the Law of Moses.

Paul refers to Abraham (as he does again in the Roman letter). Abraham, Paul points out, was approved of and accepted by God because of his faith, before the rite of circumcision had been introduced among the Jews, and before the Law of Moses was given.

Paul imagines the recipients of his letter asking, 'Why was the law given?' He explains that while the law sets right standards it also exposes people's failure to fulfil its demands.

Such fulfilment is only possible through faith in the redeeming work of Christ, who brings both Jew and Gentile into one Christian fellowship.

Paul comes to his main theme – 'Freedom in Christ' – in chapter 5. His converts are called to true freedom in Christ, but if they accept circumcision they are showing themselves as slaves. Circumcision is not essential, and as for the law, it is surely summed up in one sentence: 'Love your neighbour as yourself.'

Paul contrasts the sinful practices of unredeemed human nature with what he calls the fruit of the Spirit. God's Spirit, he says, must now control their lives and enable them to bear one another's burdens, as the law of Christ requires.

Before concluding the letter, Paul takes the pen from the hand of the one who is writing and adds a postscript in 'big letters' – a final outburst of condemnation on those who would impose circumcision.

As for those who seek to discredit him, he writes, let them see the scars inflicted on his body by his persecutors. These are the proof, if required, of his utter devotion to Christ.

EPHESIANS

PAUL'S letter to the Ephesians is the first of four letters he wrote while in prison, probably in Rome while awaiting the trial before Caesar mentioned in Acts 25:12.

Ephesus was the capital city of the Roman province of Asia, near the coast and on an important trade route. It contained a temple to the goddess Artemis, sometimes called Diana. Paul's exciting three-year stay during his third missionary journey is chronicled in Acts 19, with his moving farewell address to the Ephesian elders found in chapter 20.

The footnote to the first verse in the *Good News Bible* and some other translations suggests that several copies of this letter may have circulated in the churches, the destination being inserted at the beginning. This may explain the absence of any personal Ephesian references, and why Paul writes, 'Since I heard of your faith . . .' (1:15).

The letter divides into two parts. In chapters 1 to 3 Paul discusses aspects of Christian belief, while in the remaining chapters he gives guidance on Christian conduct.

The dominant note of the first part of the letter is one of thanksgiving for the abundance of God's gifts to believers, and for their exercise of true faith in Jesus. Paul is moved to pray that their minds might be opened to receive God's promises and that they might know his power to enable them to live worthily.

Writing mainly to Gentiles, Paul describes what he calls 'God's secret plan', now made known through Christ. This is namely that the Gentiles – previously 'apart, at enmity, far away from God' – have now, along with believing Jews, become 'one new people' and members of the family of God. Paul concludes this part of the letter with a second prayer. In this he asks that Christ might live in their hearts, giving life a firm foundation and ensuring their growth in likeness to Christ. God's power can achieve this, and far more.

The second part of the letter opens with a challenging theme: live a life that measures up to God's standard. There are qualities of character to cultivate, and gifts to employ in the service of the Church (chapter 4). As Christ is the Light of the world, so they are to live (walk) in that light, avoiding the works of darkness (chapter 5). Human relationships – husbands with wives, children with parents, slaves with masters – are to be conducted in accordance with Christian principles (chapters 5 and 6).

Finally, Paul addresses them as 'soldiers of Christ', clothing them, in allegorical fashion, with equipment required for defence against 'the devil's evil tricks' and for fighting the Lord's battles.

He concludes by introducing Tychicus – who will carry the letter to its destination – before commending them all to God's grace.

PHILIPPIANS

PAUL'S second letter from prison breathes an atmosphere of affection and joy as he writes to one of his best-loved Christian communities – the congregation at Philippi.

Since the days of that church's dramatic beginnings, witnessed and described by Luke in Acts 16, its members have given practical help and support to Paul on his journeys. Indeed, his reason for writing now is to thank them for help yet again. The letter is to be conveyed to them by Epaphroditus, one of their number.

Paul says he has all he needs and in the power of Christ is ready to face whatever happens, but he is moved by their kindness.

Such sentiments are also expressed in Paul's moving prayer, at the beginning of the letter, that the Philippian Christians' love for others may continue and expand, so that – free from impurity and blame – they can await 'the day of Christ' with confidence.

Paul goes on to comment on his own current experience. He concludes that his imprisonment has been beneficial, not only because the whole palace community in Rome has heard about him, but also because Christians are being encouraged by his example.

He wonders about the future. Will he live on, or face death after his trial? Though Paul is not sure which he prefers, he believes he should remain among them for a while to encourage them.

In chapter 2, urging his readers to develop the gifts of compassion and humility, Paul describes, in memorable words, the example of Jesus. Hundreds of years later Charles Wesley was to express these thoughts in a hymn still sung around the world:

> *He left his Father's throne above,*
> *So free, so infinite his grace,*
> *Emptied himself of all but love*
> *And bled for Adam's helpless race.*

The example of Jesus was surely a challenge to the Christians at Philippi to work steadily towards God's desire for them to be his perfect children, shining as lights in a dark world.

Though Paul might not see them for some time, he hopes to send Timothy, whom he commends highly, to visit them. And, of course, Epaphroditus – who was ill but has now recovered – will soon return to them, bearing this letter.

In chapter 3 Paul issues a stern warning against the kind of false teaching – highlighted in the Galatian letter – which may have surfaced in Philippi. He repeats the statement made in 2 Corinthians 11 that though he is as much a Jew as anyone, this is not as important as knowing Christ. This remains the supreme goal of his life.

In chapter 4 a personal appeal to two women members of the church to resolve their quarrel is followed by exhortations to cultivate joyfulness, reject worry and receive God's peace as guardian of their hearts.

The letter closes with special greetings from 'those who belong to the Emperor's palace' (4:22, *Good News Bible*). Prisoner Paul has not been idle while awaiting trial before Caesar.

COLOSSIANS

THERE are obvious similarities between Paul's letter to the Colossians and the one he writes to the Ephesians. Both are written during Paul's imprisonment, and they share some topics.

Both are entrusted to the same messenger, Tychicus, who also carries a third letter, addressed to Philemon, who may have lived in Colossae. (What a precious bundle Tychicus carried in his knapsack!)

As in his letter to the Ephesians, Paul begins his Colossian letter with thanksgiving for what he has heard of the faith of the Christians in that city.

He then moves naturally into prayer for them, that they might be filled with knowledge of God's will, live in obedience to him and find strength to endure hardship with patience and God-given joy.

Paul insists that, though they do not know him personally, the Colossian Christians are part of the whole Church which is his concern, for which he endures suffering and to whom he declares God's 'secret plan' of salvation through Christ.

Paul warns of dangers to be faced – partly, as elsewhere, from those seeking to impose on Gentiles such Jewish customs as circumcision, restrictive food laws and participation in Jewish festivals.

Other false teaching springs from pagan philosophy which questions the supremacy of Jesus and requires Christians to impose severe disciplines on themselves to control their wayward nature.

Paul's response is, firstly, to present an exalted picture of Christ, who is 'the visible likeness of the invisible God' through whom God has planned to 'bring the whole universe back to himself' (1:15, 20, all references from the *Good News Bible*).

Paul then challenges both false Jewish teachers and pagan philosophers with the truth that the redemptive power of Jesus brings new life to believers, so that restrictive rules and new philosophies are superseded. Paul calls upon the Colossian Christians to live out their new life in Christ, putting to death all earthly passions and desires, and clothing themselves with Christlike qualities (described in his letter to the Galatians as the 'fruit of the Spirit') – especially love, which 'binds all things together in perfect unity' (3:14). Such qualities, says Paul, will enhance all human relationships: wives with husbands, children with parents, slaves with masters.

Chapter 4 contains final instructions and interesting references to various people. Included is a moving tribute to Epaphras, perhaps the founder of their church, who is now in Rome with Paul.

Note the reference to a Laodician letter (presumably lost), also Paul's personal signature, together with his heartfelt plea: 'Do not forget my chains!'

FIRST LETTER TO THE THESSALONIANS

FOR Paul's First Letter to the Thessalonians we return to his second missionary journey. Having successfully established the first European church, in Philippi, Paul moves on, accompanied by Silas and Timothy, to Thessalonica, capital of the Roman province of Macedonia.

Acts 17 provides a brief account of the stormy beginnings of this church. Because of the circumstances, it is deemed wise for Paul to leave under cover of night.

Later, while in Athens, Paul sends Timothy back to Thessalonica to find out how things are going. The report, received by Paul in Corinth, to where he has moved, is an encouraging one.

Paul responds by writing this letter. In chapter 3 he recounts some of the details and adds one of his typical prayers.

Paul begins his letter by reflecting with much thanksgiving on the eager reception given by the Thessalonians to the Christian message. As a result, news of their faith has spread through the surrounding country.

Paul says he and his companions visited them with the purest motives – no tricks, no flattering talk, but deep sincerity, demonstrated by their working day and night so as not to burden the church.

Paul comments on the persecution he and his companions had endured, and notes the Thessalonians are also facing stern opposition from Jewish opponents of the gospel.

Paul wishes he could visit them again to strengthen their faith. So far, though, he has been prevented.

Urging them to live a truly godly life, Paul returns in chapter 4 to the subject of sexual immorality, about which he has earlier instructed them. Holiness of life, which is God's purpose for them, requires the highest standards in all areas of life. Paul commends them for their spirit of loving fellowship to each another, which is earning the respect of unbelievers.

Finally, Paul speaks about the return to earth of the risen and ascended Lord, to reign over his people (several brief allusions to this have already appeared in the letter – see 1:10, 2:19, 3:13).

The Thessalonian Christians are asking important questions such as, 'What about the Christians who have already died?'

At this point in his ministry it seems Paul believes he will still be alive to witness Jesus' return. But those who have died will not miss out. Paul says they will be raised to life first, then 'we who are still living' will join them and be with the glorified Christ for ever.

As to the question of when all this will happen, Paul gives the same answer Jesus gave – the time is unknown. All Christians need to know is that it will happen suddenly and unexpectedly. Their task, therefore, is to be alert and disciplined, protected as Christian soldiers by the armour of faith and hope and love.

A final collection of brief exhortations, especially to cultivate holiness of 'spirit, soul and body', bring this early letter of Paul to a close.

SECOND LETTER TO THE THESSALONIANS

A LETTER from a distant friend is always welcome, but if another quickly follows, one is likely to wonder what has happened.

So, we might ask, what has happened at Thessalonica to warrant a second letter from Paul so soon?

Misunderstanding has arisen among believers about the return of the risen and glorified Christ. Paul wonders if his first letter was the cause, or if someone has sent a letter falsely claiming it to be from him.

For whatever reason, word has spread that 'the day of the Lord' has already taken place.

After the usual greetings and thanksgiving for the faith of the Thessalonian Christians in the face of increasing persecution, Paul begins his reply in chapter 2.

He strongly refutes the rumour, declaring that the return of Christ will not take place until certain things have happened. What things are they? Paul's explanation is far from easy to understand. For one thing, he adopts a special kind of picture language sometimes used by Jewish writers when discussing matters to do with the spiritual world.

For example, he refers in verse 7 to the 'Mysterious Wickedness' (all quotations from the *Good News Bible*) which is already at work in the world – and still is today.

In the same verse he mentions 'the one who holds it back'. We do not know for sure what he means, but the influence of godly people throughout the world, backed by the power of the Holy Spirit, surely does help to restrain the advance of evil.

Eventually, Paul declares, the 'Wicked One' (mentioned three times in these verses) will be unmasked and revealed for what he is, perhaps causing for a time an intensifying of evil activity in the world.

If and when that happens, Christians are assured of the appearance of Christ, who will destroy the power of evil once and for all. (The words of Jesus as recorded in Luke 21:28 are relevant here.)

Turning from this solemn subject, Paul gives thanks that those to whom he is writing have been chosen by God to be saved and become his holy people. He prays that they may be granted 'unfailing courage and a firm hope ... to always do and say what is good' (2:16, 17).

Before concluding this letter Paul turns to a down-to-earth subject. In his first letter to them he urged the Thessalonians to 'warn the idle' (5:14). Now he re-emphasises this, warning them against 'some people among you who live lazy lives and who do nothing except meddle in other people's business' (3:11).

Do they, perhaps, think work can cease now the return of Christ is at hand?

Paul's censure is brief and to the point. Do they not recall Paul's previous declaration that whoever refuses to work is not allowed to eat? Orderliness and industry are to be hallmarks of their life together.

In case he has been too harsh in his condemnation Paul reminds the Thessalonians that such offenders are to be treated not as enemies but as brothers. And so, following a moving benediction of peace, Paul – a tireless correspondent – signs off once again.

FIRST LETTER TO TIMOTHY

THE next three New Testament books are letters written to Timothy and Titus, two of Paul's trusted lieutenants.

They are sometimes called 'pastoral' letters, coming as they do from one who is writing as a pastor, or shepherd, of a Christian community.

These letters are very different from those we have already studied in our progress through the New Testament.

In fact they are so different that some scholars wonder whether Paul really wrote them or, if he did, if he was released from prison for a time, undertaking another missionary journey (not mentioned in the Acts of the Apostles) and visiting places mentioned in the letter to Titus. Evidence on both matters is inconclusive, so we accept Paul's authorship here while regarding the second question as an interesting but unproven theory.

Timothy is a young man whose mother is a Jewess and father a Gentile. He travelled with Paul on his second missionary journey, and is in Ephesus when this letter is written.

Paul wants him to remain there to combat false teaching and oppose those who are spreading it.

The subject surfaces several times in the letter. Indeed, two members of the church are named as having an unworthy influence. They are to be barred from the fellowship.

Church worship is the subject in chapter 2, with emphasis on public prayer.

Paul does not want women to take part in this. They are to be content to worship in silence, to dress soberly, do good deeds and bear children. The reason given is not very convincing!

Local leadership is the subject of chapter 3 and seems to be of two kinds.

The *Good News Bible* describes those responsible as 'church leaders' and 'church helpers'. It seems their present-day equivalents are vicars and curates, or ministers and deacons.

All are to be of good character, married to one wife, good husbands and fathers, not new converts, and of good reputation outside the church.

Much personal advice is offered to Timothy in chapter 4 and elsewhere.

His youthfulness must not hinder his ministry. While physical exercise is of some value, spiritual development is all-important. Later, Paul refers to Timothy as often being ill, and advises 'a little wine' to assist digestion.

In chapter 5 Paul urges great sensitivity in relationships with church members, young and old, male and female.

Specifically, Paul gives instructions regarding widows in the church. In verses 11 to 15 young widows are, as we say, given a rather bad press! But older widows who prove their worth can be used in service and receive support.

In chapter 6 Paul warns of the danger of aiming for earthly riches, declaring that the love of money is the source of many evils. He urges the wealthy to be generous in the service of others.

Finally the ageing apostle appeals to his young assistant, 'Timothy, keep safe what has been entrusted to your care' (6:20, *GNB*).

So concludes a brief but fascinating picture of life in a first-century Christian church.

SECOND LETTER TO TIMOTHY

THE second letter to Timothy is followed in the New Testament by two further letters of Paul, but this one is clearly the last to be written.

Paul is in prison, lonely and with only Luke as companion. Paul has undergone a first interrogation by his Roman captors and, though successfully defending himself, has no illusions about the final outcome. 'The hour has come for me to be sacrificed,' he writes (4:6, all references from the *Good News Bible*).

Like the athlete mentioned earlier in the letter, he has performed well in the race of life and has 'run the full distance' (4:7).

Paul believes the Lord will reward his faithfulness, as he does for all who remain true to the end. Earlier in the letter Paul uses the opportunity to counsel his young assistant, Timothy, reminding him of the rich heritage of faith passed on by his mother and grandmother.

Paul urges this sometimes timid and over-sensitive leader to be courageous in proclaiming the truth Paul taught him.

In chapter 2 the apostle uses a number of images to describe the kind of service Christians should aim for: the single-minded obedience of the soldier; the disciplined acceptance of the rules of the race as athletes; the hard day-and-night dedication of the farmer. Timothy is urged to be an unashamed and devoted worker, or – using another image – to be like a utensil made of precious metal, clean and ready for the owner's special use.

Understandably for one facing martyrdom, the subject of suffering for Christ's sake features prominently in this letter. Paul reminds Timothy of what happened when he visited Timothy's home town of Lystra, and other towns nearby. Everyone who proposes to live a godly life in Christ will face persecution, concludes Paul. So Timothy is to study the Scriptures, which were inspired by God and taught to him from his youth. They will equip him and those he teaches for sacrificial service.

There are difficult days ahead for the Church. A general deterioration in standards of behaviour will not leave the Church untouched. Some people, while displaying an outward form of religion, will lack genuine power from God. Others will turn to false doctrines or to teachers who tell them only what they want to hear.

Names of deserters or false teachers appear in various parts of the letter. Among them is Demas, who was once a fellow-worker with Paul but who 'fell in love with this present world and . . . deserted me' (4:10). The letter ends with an urgent appeal for Timothy to hurry back to Rome, bringing a coat, much-needed to face the coming winter, and some books and parchments left behind at Troas.

Paul tells Timothy to bring Mark with him, to 'help me in the work'. The end may be near, but Paul plans to keep working to the last.

TITUS

TITUS is not mentioned by name in the Acts of the Apostles. Indeed, we know about him only through the letters of Paul.

From Galatians (2:1-4) we learn he is a Greek. This leads some Jewish Christians to call for him to be circumcised.

Paul disagrees and takes Titus with him to Jerusalem, where some of the Christian leaders uphold Paul's stand. They agree that Gentile Christians need not conform to such Jewish practices.

It is during Paul's difficulties with the church at Corinth that Titus proves his value.

In Paul's second letter to the Corinthians Titus's name appears nine times, including references to what are probably three separate visits to Corinth.

The first visit was to organise a collection for needy Christians in Jerusalem, the second was to take a so-called 'severe letter' which caused Paul acute anxiety, and the third was to complete the collection referred to.

From Paul's letter to his valuable assistant we learn that Titus is on the island of Crete, where Paul left him to organise the churches and appoint local leadership.

In terms similar to those used in his first letter to Timothy, Paul outlines the qualities to look for when appointing such leaders.

At the same time he warns that the Cretans may well prove difficult to handle, quoting an uncomplimentary remark by one of their own prophets.

It is therefore important for Titus to expose and refute all erroneous teaching and insist on upright behaviour, whether from older men and women, younger members of the congregation or from slaves, who must submit to their masters and be a credit to the cause of Christ.

The kind of sound teaching which Titus is to provide is outlined in 2:11-14 and 3:4-7.

At the close of his letter Paul reveals his plans for some of his helpers. Titus is to be replaced by either Artemas or Tychicus. When that happens Titus is to travel to Nicopolis, on the west coast of Macedonia, where Paul intends to spend the winter.

Two others – Zenas (of whom we know nothing) and Apollos (whose eloquence attracted attention in Ephesus and Corinth) – are to be assisted on their way, though where they are to go is not indicated.

It looks as if Paul, himself a hardened traveller, believes in keeping his troops on the move.

PHILEMON

OUR study of Paul's correspondence concludes with a delightful personal letter to a friend and Christian brother living in Colossae.

Philemon, a man of some wealth, in whose house Christians meet together (verse 2), has been led to Christ by Paul's ministry – not in Colossae, which he had not yet visited, but probably in Ephesus during Paul's three-year stay there.

Onesimus, a slave belonging to Philemon, escapes to Rome after robbing his master. Worried and frightened by the possible consequences, he searches for his master's friend Paul, whom he knows is in prison somewhere in the city.

He finds Paul, seeks his help, and becomes a Christian. In turn, Paul befriends the young man.

Eventually Onesimus must return to Colossae and, as we say, 'face the music'. So when Tychicus is preparing to travel to the area with letters for Ephesus and Colossae, Paul composes a third letter, entrusting both it and the converted (and no doubt apprehensive) slave to the messenger's care.

In the letter, Paul appeals to Philemon to receive Onesimus back into his household, not just as a slave but as a 'dear brother in Christ' (verse 16, all references from the *Good News Bible*).

In a play on the meaning of the name 'Onesimus' ('useful'), he claims that the one who had been 'of no use' to his master has, by receiving Christ, become 'useful' (verse 11). Indeed, his absence from his master 'for a short time' has prepared him to give much better service 'for all time' (verse 15).

While Paul acknowledges his own affection for Onesimus and his appreciation of his valued service, he sends him back in the hope that Philemon will 'welcome him back just as you would welcome me' (verse 17).

The apostle promises to refund whatever Onesimus has stolen, though he reminds his friend of the debt of gratitude he owes Paul for leading him to Christ (verse 19)!

Here we see the great apostle at his best, personally affectionate towards fellow Christians, whether slaves or masters, and deeply involved in the work of the Lord as he leads another prodigal back to the Father's house.

HEBREWS

THE title of this letter refers to a particular group of Jewish Christians, perhaps living in Rome.

Some years have passed since they established their church, and comparatively few Jews have accepted Christ as the promised Messiah and joined their congregation.

With opposition increasing, many members of this group are strongly tempted to renounce their new faith and return to Judaism. This letter is therefore written to stress again the supremacy of Christ in God's plan of redemption.

The name of the writer is not known. Paul's name was linked with it, but doubts about this were expressed as far back as the third century AD.

Whoever the writer is, he reveals a wide knowledge of the Old Testament and quotes freely from a selection of its books.

Though referred to as a letter, the Book of Hebrews is better described as a written sermon or treatise, to the end of which a brief greeting is added.

The short prologue (verses 1 to 3) sets out the writer's claim that through God's Son, Jesus, God has spoken his latest and greatest message to the world.

Then references to various Jewish beliefs and practices occupy the first 10 chapters.

Angels, for example, figure much in Jewish thought. Yes, Jesus was made 'for a little while lower than the angels' in coming to earth and suffering death like a human being; but now he is 'crowned . . . with glory and honour' (2:7, all quotations from the *Good News Bible*).

Next, Moses is acknowledged as God's faithful servant, but Jesus, as God's Son, is greater (3:2-6).

The most prominent theme is of Jesus as eternal high priest. Through his death – the perfect sacrifice for sin – Jesus replaces once and for all the yearly atonement sacrifices of Temple ritual.

They were the 'shadow' or promise, while Jesus is the 'substance' or fulfilment of God's redemptive purpose (8:5-6).

Jesus also fulfils Jeremiah's promise, quoted in chapter 8, of a better covenant to take the place of the Mosaic covenant of Law which had proved so ineffective.

Scattered throughout these chapters are earnest appeals: to hold on to their faith, to draw nearer to Christ, to move forward with him. Warnings of the consequences of rejection are also given (eg 10:19-39).

The last three chapters are more straightforward.

The 'grand parade' of heroes of the faith in chapter 11 is followed by the challenge, in chapter 12, to emulate such faith by running life's race with eyes steadily fixed on Jesus.

Suffering may come the believer's way, but God is aware of it, and regards it like a father's discipline of his sons, to strengthen their resolve (12:7-11).

Various instructions and exhortations bring this long treatise to a close, including the reminder that 'Jesus Christ is the same yesterday, today, and for ever' (13:8). A careful reading of this challenging book will reveal many gems of truth like that!

JAMES

FOUR people, two of them apostles, bear the name James in the New Testament. The writer of this letter – the first of the so-called 'general' letters – is thought to have been the brother of Jesus mentioned in Mark 6:3. Despite sharing his family's lack of belief in Jesus' mission during his earthly life, James becomes a Christian – perhaps through a meeting with the risen Christ, as recorded by Paul (1 Corinthians 15:7). Later James presides over the church at Jerusalem and, it is believed, suffers a martyr's death in AD 62.

The letter of James has been described as an 'ethical scrapbook'. Ethical because its subject is Christian conduct and behaviour, and scrapbook because of its lack of an orderly arrangement in its subject matter. The language at times recalls the style of Old Testament Wisdom literature (such as the Book of Proverbs), but a touch of prophetic fervour here and there suggests to one commentator that James is 'the Amos of the New Testament'. There are also many reminders of the teaching of Jesus. Not surprisingly, the letter begins with a call to faithfulness under trial, which the Church is beginning to experience. Such trial, declares James, is to be expected and faced with courage, even joy! He distinguishes such trials, which are tests of faithfulness, from temptations, which arise from within and must be resisted (1:12-15).

Chapter 2 begins with a warning against the kind of prejudice which looks down on poor people while showing special favour to those who are rich. The law of the Kingdom, to be applied to all, is 'love your neighbour as you love yourself' (2:8, *Good News Bible*). In the same chapter, James insists that faith and works (actions) are not opposites. Yes, salvation is received by faith alone, but it will be confirmed by the righteous actions which follow (2:22).

The dangerous power of the tongue is highlighted in chapter 3, where it is likened to a bit in a horse's mouth, a rudder which steers a great ship, and a tiny flame which can set a whole forest ablaze. How important it is, therefore, that the heart be filled with 'the wisdom from above', so producing a 'harvest of good deeds' (3:17, *GNB*)! Chapters 4 and 5 both begin in prophetic style, with strong condemnations of the craze for material possessions and earthly riches.

Echoing the words of Jesus in the Sermon on the Mount (Matthew 6:19-21), James warns of the 'moths' which devour the garment and 'rust' which eats away the silver and gold.

The letter concludes in a calmer atmosphere as the writer appeals for patient endurance, and commends the practice of believing prayer, especially in times of trouble and sickness. In a postscript, James urges the reader to take special care of anyone tempted to turn aside from the faith. Saving such a person yields lasting riches indeed!

FIRST LETTER OF PETER

WE now reach the first of two letters from a prominent member of Jesus' 12 disciples – Simon Peter, the big fisherman Jesus called from his boats and nets to become a 'fisher of men' for the Kingdom of God.

From the letter's closing verses we learn that Peter is in Rome (code-named Babylon, a place with bitter memories for Jews). With him is Silas, whose help with the letter Peter acknowledges.

Peter begins by greeting 'God's chosen people' living in various provinces in Asia Minor. There follows a magnificent opening call to thanksgiving for the 'living hope' which God has provided through Jesus, with rich blessings in store for his people in due time.

Three basic themes can be traced through these chapters.

Firstly, 'many kinds of trials' are to be expected, but 'only for a while'. The trials will enable the Christians to prove their faith is genuine, just as fire is applied to gold to test its purity.

God recognises and blesses such 'undeserved' suffering, which should be accepted in a spirit of thankfulness that those suffering are found worthy to bear Christ's name as Christians.

Secondly, Jesus is the great example, enduring costly suffering like 'a lamb without defect or flaw', meeting every trial without threats or insults, and placing his hope firmly in God. Christians should follow in his steps.

Thirdly, the Christian life involves obedience to God, rejection of former lifestyles and adoption of the way of holiness, which will show itself in sincere love for others.

It will also enrich every human relationship, such as those of slaves with masters and husbands with wives. This is especially crucial where one partner is not a Christian.

Indeed, Christian conduct is to be shown towards all non-Christians, including those in authority. Questions about faith should always be answered with gentleness and respect.

Two other passages contribute to the riches of this letter.

In the first 10 verses of chapter 2 Peter draws on his knowledge of Old Testament Scripture to present Christ as 'the living stone' rejected by unbelievers but now revealed as the very cornerstone of God's plan for mankind.

And in the first four verses of chapter 5 Peter assumes the mantle of the shepherd, of which Jesus spoke to him by Lake Galilee (see John 21:15-17).

Peter challenges all church elders to be faithful shepherds, caring in love for the sheep entrusted to them, so that when the Chief Shepherd appears they will receive the unfading crown of glory.

THE SECOND LETTER OF PETER

THE second letter of Peter is included among the New Testament's 'general' letters – which is fitting, as it is addressed to Christians everywhere.

After a brief greeting, Peter begins by declaring that God has provided for his people 'everything we need to live a truly religious life' (1:3, all quotations from the *Good News Bible*).

Christians are to build upon this by developing various qualities which will make them effective witnesses for Christ, with the right to enter his eternal Kingdom.

Peter's expectation that he is soon to 'put off this mortal body' adds urgency to his words. He states that his authority stems from having seen the Lord, especially on the Mount of Transfiguration, when he heard God's voice confirming Jesus' divine Sonship. The readers of his letter should therefore heed the message, which is 'like a lamp shining in a dark place' (1:19).

The mood changes in chapter 2, with a stern denunciation of the activities of false teachers who have never turned away from the immoral life of the world and who now seek to trap the unwary with their 'made-up stories'.

Judgement will surely come upon them, as it did in Noah's time, and also when Sodom and Gomorrah were destroyed. The story of Balaam the soothsayer (Numbers 22) is also quoted as further illustration of God's intervention to prevent wrong-doing.

The note of condemnation grows more strident: these men are like wild animals, like dried-up springs. They promise freedom while they themselves are slaves to destructive habits.

Finally, a subject causing controversy in the Church at that time occupies chapter 3: the return of Jesus Christ to earth, an event known as 'the day of the Lord'.

Some are openly mocking about this, saying, 'Where is he? Our fathers have already died, but everything is still the same!' (3:4).

Peter, in reply, quotes from Psalm 90, declaring that one day is as a thousand years with God. If Jesus' return is delayed, it is to give people more opportunity to repent.

With vivid imagery Peter paints a lurid picture of the happenings which will accompany the promised event, and urges his readers to practise holiness of life as they wait for the fulfilment of God's promise. He refers to Paul's writings on the subject; they include 'some difficult things' which are falsely interpreted by ignorant and unstable people.

The letter ends with a final warning and a call to 'grow in the grace and knowledge of our Lord and Saviour Jesus Christ' (3:18).

FIRST LETTER OF JOHN

THE study relating to the Gospel of John made reference to another John, known as 'The Elder', who may have compiled the Gospel from the aged apostle's memories. Many factors lead to the conclusion that the same person compiled this letter.

There are a number of similarities between the two writings.

The main subjects tackled in the letter are based on key words already familiar in the Gospel.

God is light. Thus we are called to 'live in the light', enjoying rich fellowship with each other and experiencing forgiveness from sin.

God (Christ) is righteous. The onus is therefore on Christians to reject sin and do what is right.

God is love. The word 'love' is used so often it becomes the overall theme of the letter. Here it is described as the love of a father for his children.

Recognising this truth motivates us to put away sin and keep ourselves pure. Such love should inspire within the Christian family a spirit of love for each other in which needs are recognised and action taken to help.

We are reminded that the proof of such love is that Jesus came and died as Saviour for our sins.This can give us freedom from fear, and courage to face the future.

Two further subjects call for comment.

False teaching of a particular kind is spreading in Ephesus. Based on the view that true religion is of the spirit, it regards the flesh as inherently evil, which means that Jesus could not have been truly human, though he may have seemed so.

To accept this would deny that Jesus really died for our sins and rose again. John refutes this heresy, stressing both the divinity and humanity of Jesus.

The word 'world' is used, both in the Gospel and in the letter, as referring to the ungodly world of darkness and sin.

The disciples, said Jesus, were 'not of this world', and John's letter urges Christians not to love this world, which has alienated itself from God and is passing away.

Finally, note the phrase 'eternal life'. This is common to both Gospel and letter and means not just 'life after death' but also 'life of eternal quality' to be enjoyed here and now.

SECOND AND THIRD LETTERS OF JOHN

THE two short letters known as the second and third letters of John are written by 'The Elder'. He is almost certainly the 'other' John referred to in the previous studies relating to the first letter of John and the Gospel of John.

Note in the letters the description of Christians as those who 'know the truth' and who 'live in the truth' (2 John 1, 4 and 3 John 3, 4, *Good News Bible*).

It's thought the 'dear Lady' to whom the second letter is addressed is in fact a church. Perhaps it is a coded reference, to avoid giving the church's location at a time when Christians were in danger of persecution. This would mean the 'children' are the members of the congregation.

Themes from John's first letter are repeated, including the call to obey God's commands – especially to 'love one another' (verse 5).

There is a warning about the special kind of false teaching which denies the true humanity of Jesus. Such teachers are not to be welcomed into the homes of believers, nor even greeted with the words, 'Peace be with you' (verse 10). What they are doing is evil.

The letter is short, as John hopes to visit them soon and speak to them personally.

The final greeting is in the same code, 'The children of your dear Sister' presumably referring to members of the church to which John belongs.

The recipient of the third letter is named as Gaius, who is probably a prominent member of the church to which the second letter is addressed.

Gaius is praised for showing hospitality to a group of travelling evangelists. These people had spoken of their gratitude to John when he met them, and John here expresses his pleasure at this.

But Diotrephes, who is referred to next, and who has pretensions to leadership, refused to give such hospitality to travellers and even prevented others from doing so. John adds that he has been saying terrible things about them, commenting: 'The lies he tells!' (verse 10).

A third person, Demetrius, is also mentioned, this time with commendation, because everyone speaks well of him, including John himself.

This brief insight into the personalities and problems of life in this growing church reminds us that the Kingdom is growing in the world of real people, whose 'human-ness' is often apparent.

JUDE

THE writer of this last letter in the New Testament is believed to be Jude (or Judas), one of the younger brothers of Jesus mentioned in Mark 6:3. He does not claim to be an apostle and gives no indication as to the destination of the letter, although the wording of verse 5 suggests he may have Gentile Christians in mind.

Setting out to compose a straightforward description of the way of salvation, Jude changes direction in verse 3, after receiving disturbing news about the activities of 'some godless people' who have 'slipped in unnoticed among us, persons who distort the message' (verse 4, all references from the *Good News Bible*).

It is the Christian principle of 'freedom in Christ' which is being distorted, becoming, in the hands of such teachers, licence to indulge in immoral practices.

Jude selects a number of illustrations from Jewish history – including two from Jewish writings not in the Bible – to show the severity of God's judgement as meted out to past offenders. Note the similarity here with the second chapter of 2 Peter, where Peter may be quoting from Jude.

These false teachers try to blame others for the divisions they themselves are causing in the Church. Meanwhile they use boasting and flattery to achieve their aims.

Vivid descriptions of their ungodly behaviour are given, especially in verses 11 to 13. The writer then addresses his Christian friends. He urges them to recall the warnings of Jesus as conveyed by the apostles, and to build upon the faith they already possess.

Jude appeals to them to 'keep yourselves in the love of God' (verse 21) while, in the spirit of Jesus, showing mercy towards doubters.

If necessary, they should take stern measures to rescue those who are deceived and drawn into sin.

The Methodist hymn writer Charles Wesley describes the spirit in which such actions should be taken:

To hate the sin with all my heart,
But still the sinner love.

And so to the lovely benediction, which is worthy to take its place at the conclusion not just of this letter but of all the New Testament letters. 'To him who is able to keep you from falling . . .' (verse 24). Or, as early-day Salvationists sang:

He will keep you from falling,
*   He will keep to the end;*
What a Saviour is Jesus!
*   What a wonderful friend!*

REVELATION

THE Book of Daniel and the Book of Revelation are two biblical examples of a special kind of written prophecy known as Apocalyptic Literature. Other examples, not included in the Bible, appear among Jewish writings during the period between the Old and New Testaments.

Writings like these emerge at times when God's people, Jews or Christians, are facing persecution.

Their purpose is to encourage believers to hold on to their faith in the assurance that, although the present situation seems dark, God is still in control. The day will come when he will honour his people's faithfulness, overthrow his enemies and usher in a new and glorious era of peace and joy.

Special features of this kind of writing include the use of highly dramatic dreams and visions – often peopled by animals, monsters or angels – together with the symbolic use of numbers. By such means the writers hope to convey their message to the faithful, who will recognise the hidden 'code'. The code, however, will make the writing meaningless to the enemy if a copy falls into their hands.

Towards the close of the first century AD, Roman emperors, faced with the problem of controlling their vast empire, introduced the concept of emperor worship. They set up statues of themselves, appointed priests to officiate, and issued edicts compelling subject peoples to accord them divine honours.

It was a time of deep challenge to Christians, whose allegiance can be given only to the one true God. Many refused to obey such an order, choosing to suffer a martyr's death rather than be unfaithful to their Lord.

The Book of Revelation first appears during this period of grave peril for the young Church. The writer is named as 'John, your brother', and is believed by many to be the apostle John, who at that time was exiled on the island of Patmos, by order of the Emperor Domitian, as a punishment for proclaiming God's word.

When reading this remarkable work, we should avoid the temptation to look for a literal interpretation of all its details. It is wrong, for example, to attempt to discover the exact date and circumstances of the expected return of Christ.

The broad message of the book is of the cosmic struggle between Satanic evil and the God-directed forces of goodness, with the triumphant certainty of the final overthrow of Satan and the establishment of the everlasting Kingdom of God.

In the first chapter of Revelation, the writer introduces himself, explains where he is and why, greets the seven Asian churches and describes his initial vision of the glorified Christ.

Those seven churches are now presented with a kind of heavenly 'interim report' on the quality and effectiveness of their witness. Assessments vary, from 'wholly praiseworthy' to 'regrettably unworthy'.

In spite of this, each church is given a conditional promise of future blessing 'to those who win the victory'.

The first great vision of the heavenly realm reveals the throne of God, surrounded by 24 elders and four strange 'living creatures'.

A seven-sealed Scroll of Judgement is produced and handed to the Lamb (representing Christ), who alone is worthy to open it. Meanwhile, countless thousands of angels sing 'a new song'.

There now follows a series of forbidding visions of judgement, including the breaking of the seven seals, the successive blowing of seven trumpets, and the pouring out upon the earth by angels of seven bowls containing plagues.

Deadly conflicts take place between God and Satan, one result of which is the destruction of the city and empire of Rome – code-named Babylon.

However, not all is gloom and doom in these central chapters. Judgements are interrupted from time to time with glimpses of the glories of Heaven.

Eventually the dark clouds of struggle and judgement begin to lift. A strange vision is inserted of 1,000 years of peace, with Satan chained and imprisoned, and Christ ruling over the earth. This ends with the release and final destruction of Satan, and the setting-up of the 'great white throne' for the Day of Judgement.

The two closing chapters present a heart-warming vision of the 'new Heaven and new earth', together with an extended description of the Holy City – New Jerusalem – shining in the light of the glory of God.

Its gates are open to receive all whose names are in the book of life, but closed to every kind of sin and impurity. Its river of life flows to provide healing for the nations.

Though difficult to understand at times, passages from this book have provided comfort and hope for many people in times of sorrow and bereavement. From its pages also come words used in Handel's great oratorio, *Messiah*:

Worthy is the lamb that was slain to receive power and riches and wisdom and strength and honour and glory and blessing!

Hallelujah! For the Lord God omnipotent reigneth! And he shall reign for ever and ever! King of Kings and Lord of Lords; Hallelujah!

This is the heart of the book's message, to which Handel's music bears continuing witness.

CENTURIES OF OLD TESTAMENT HISTORY
(All dates approximate)

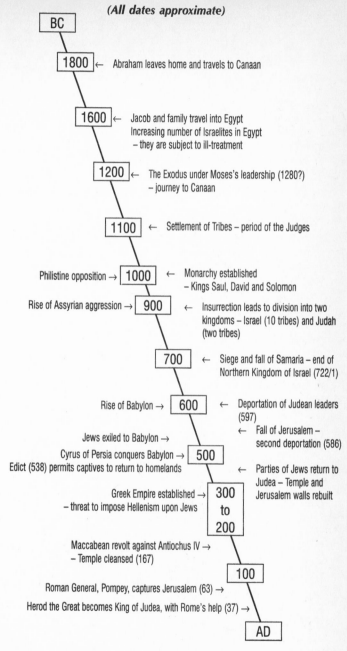

BC

1800 ← Abraham leaves home and travels to Canaan

1600 ← Jacob and family travel into Egypt
Increasing number of Israelites in Egypt
– they are subject to ill-treatment

1200 ← The Exodus under Moses's leadership (1280?)
– journey to Canaan

1100 ← Settlement of Tribes – period of the Judges

Philistine opposition → 1000 ← Monarchy established
– Kings Saul, David and Solomon

Rise of Assyrian aggression → 900 ← Insurrection leads to division into two
kingdoms – Israel (10 tribes) and Judah
(two tribes)

700 ← Siege and fall of Samaria – end of
Northern Kingdom of Israel (722/1)

Rise of Babylon → 600 ← Deportation of Judean leaders
(597)
← Fall of Jerusalem –
Jews exiled to Babylon → second deportation (586)
Cyrus of Persia conquers Babylon → 500
Edict (538) permits captives to return to homelands ← Parties of Jews return to
Judea – Temple and
Greek Empire established → 300 Jerusalem walls rebuilt
– threat to impose Hellenism upon Jews to
200

Maccabean revolt against Antiochus IV →
– Temple cleansed (167)

100

Roman General, Pompey, captures Jerusalem (63) →

Herod the Great becomes King of Judea, with Rome's help (37) →

AD

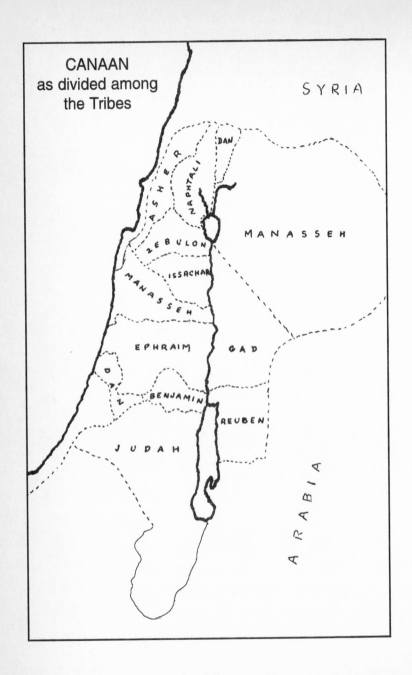

CANAAN
as divided among
the Tribes

SYRIA

ASHER

DAN

NAPHTALI

MANASSEH

ZEBULON

ISSACHAR

MANASSEH

EPHRAIM

GAD

DAN

BENJAMIN

REUBEN

JUDAH

ARABIA

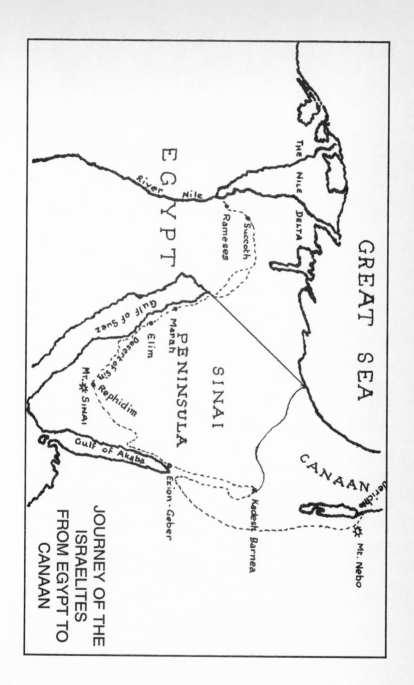

JOURNEY OF THE
ISRAELITES
FROM EGYPT TO
CANAAN

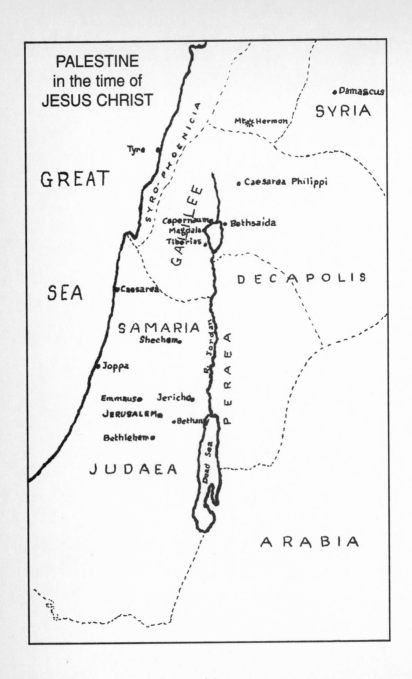

PALESTINE
in the time of
JESUS CHRIST

Damascus

SYRIA

Mt. Hermon

Tyre

GREAT

Caesarea Philippi

SYRO PHOENICIA

GALILEE

Capernaum
Magdala
Tiberias

Bethsaida

DECAPOLIS

SEA

Caesarea

SAMARIA

Shechem

R. Jordan

PERAEA

Joppa

Emmaus
JERUSALEM

Jericho

Bethlehem

Bethany

Dead Sea

JUDAEA

ARABIA

INDEX
of people referred to in
the Old Testament section of
A beginner's guide to the Bible

INDEX
of people referred to in
the New Testament section of
A beginner's guide to the Bible

A simple guide to the timetable of events in the New Testament

AD

0 – 10   *Birth of Jesus* in Bethlehem, also of John the Baptist

10 – 30 *'Jesus' hidden years'*
– only recorded event: Jesus' visit to Jerusalem at the age of 12, with his parents

30 – 33 *Jesus' public ministry*
– baptism and temptations
– calling of the 12 disciples
– teaching and healing in Galilee
– ministry in Transjordan and Judaea
– final journey to Jerusalem
– betrayal, arrest, trials, crucifixion
– resurrection and ascension
The apostles in Jerusalem
– The Day of Pentecost, anointing by the Holy Spirit
– Peter addresses the crowd
– Three thousand believers constitute the birth of the Christian Church
– Stephen, one of the seven deacons, arrested and stoned to death
– persecution and scattering of believers
– Philip preaches to Samaritans and Ethiopian official
– Peter preaches to Gentile, Cornelius
– other Christians travel to Phoenicia, Cyprus and Antioch (Syria)
– Saul (Paul) is converted, *en route* to Damascus
– Paul joins Barnabas at Antioch (Syria), believers first called Christians
– Paul and Barnabas set apart by church at Antioch for evangelistic mission

40 – 50 *Paul's first missionary journey* (accompanied by Barnabas and Mark)
– to Cyprus, Antioch (Pisidia), Iconium, Lystra, Derbe
– return to Antioch (Syria)
– to Jerusalem for first Christian Council
– letter to Galatians written?

50 – 60 *Paul's second missionary journey* (accompanied first by Silas, then by Timothy)
- to Philippi, Thessalonica, Berea, Athens, Corinth
- return to Antioch (Syria)
- letters to Thessalonians and Corinthians written

Paul's third missionary journey
- to Ephesus (three years), plus visits to churches in Greece
- return to Jerusalem with collection for the poor
- arrest, imprisonment in Caesarea (two years)
- letter to Romans written

60 – 70 *Paul and party journey to Rome*, violent storm *en route*
- first (?) imprisonment, captivity letters
- perhaps release and further travels
- Great Fire of Rome (64 AD), Nero blames Christians, many martyred
- Paul re-arrested, tried and executed
- Peter believed to have been crucified during this persecution
- letters to Ephesians, Philippians, Colossians, Philemon, Timothy and Titus, and Gospel of Mark, written

80 – 90 Gospels of Matthew and Luke probably appeared during this decade

90 – 100 John the Apostle in Ephesus
- the Gospel of John and Book of Revelation probably written during this period

Note: There is no reliable evidence as to the time of writing of the General Epistles, James, Peter, John, Jude, or the Book of Hebrews.